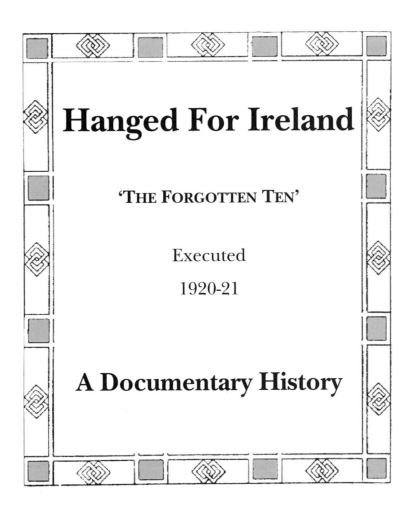

Hanged For Ireland

'THE FORGOTTEN TEN'

Executed

1920-21

A Documentary History

Tim Carey

BLACKWATER PRESS

Editor

Finola Mc Laughlin

Design, Layout and Cover

Liz Murphy

© Tim Carey 2001

ISBN 1 84131 547 8

Produced in Ireland by
Blackwater Press,
c/o Folens Publishers,
Hibernian Industrial Estate,
Greenhills Road,
Tallaght, Dublin 24.

Contents

Acknowledgements

Firstly I would like to thank TG4, Munla, whose documentary *Deichniúr Dearmada* has made this publication possible. Invaluable in this process was the assistance of Dr Tom Tracy and Sean Sherwin. I would sincerely like to thank Rosie Nic Cionnaith whose knowledge of the ten men has been of vital importance, and to Mike Keane for all his support.

A number of people gave me invaluable assistance in the writing of this book. I would especially like to thank the families of the ten men who have made available items from their family collections. I hope that they are pleased with the final product. Cara Ronan was at all times enthusiastic, diligent and thorough in assisting with the research for this book. Of course any errors or omissions are my own responsibility. I would like to thank the Minister for Justice, John O'Donoghue and Sean Aylward, Director of the Irish Prison Service. A special word of thanks also to Jim Mitchell, the Press Officer of the Irish Prison Service, for all of his help. Thanks is also due to Peter McKenna, Director, Croke Park, and the staff of the GAA Museum, Tony McGuinness, Maria Gorman, Deirdre Flood, Barry Shiel, Steven Moran and Eoin O'Driscoll and Sean McCague President of the GAA, Liam Mulvihill, Director General, and Dermot Power, Marketing Manager. Thanks also to the Council of Trustees of the National Library and the staff of the National Library, especially Theresa Biggins, Bernard Devaney and Dr Noel Kissane. I am also indebted to Kilmainham Gaol and Museum, the National Graves Association and the National Archives. Thanks are due to the *Irish Times*, Independent Newspapers, the Public Record Office, London, and the Sisters of Charity. I am also grateful to Paul Turnell, Niamh O'Sullivan, Pat Cooke and Michael Diggin. Special thanks to our childminders, my Mother, my sister Mary Kate, Áine, Phil, Corinna, Barry and Therese. However, without the absolute support and help of my wife Sinéad as usual none of this would have been possible.

October 2001

Picture Credits

The author and publisher would like to thank the following people and organisations who have supplied photographs and other images for this book.

Courtesy Doyle family: p. 113, p. 118

Courtesy Foley family: p. 135 top right, p. 163

Courtesy Hugo McVey: p. 135 bottom, p. 160, p. 189 right

Courtesy *Irish Independent*: p. 128, p. 149, p. 152, p. 156

Courtesy Irish Prison Services: p. 1, p. 48, p. 178, p. 180, p. 186, p. 191, p. 192 top, p. 193, p. 194 top, p. 203, p. 204, p. 209

Courtesy *Irish Times*: p. 81, p. 189 right

Courtesy Kilmainham Museum and Gaol: p. 11, p. 13, p. 18, p. 47, p. 51, p. 53, p. 57, p. 85, p. 91, p. 93, p. 95 top left, top right, bottom right, p. 96, p. 97, p. 100, p. 101 top & bottom, p. 102, p. 103, p. 125, p. 133, p. 137, p. 157

Courtesy Moran family: p. 68, p. 69 top & bottom

Courtesy MUNLA: p. 159

Courtesy National Library of Ireland: p. 21 Lawrence 3999, p. 35 Lawrence 1648, p. 73 Keogh 86, p. 95 bottom left Keogh 8, p. 117 Keogh 8, p. 135 top left Keogh 102, p. 138 Keogh 102, p. 161 Keogh 1635, p. 131 & p. 155 Freeman's Journal

Courtesy the *Star*: p. 192 bottom, p. 194 bottom, p. 196, p. 198

Introduction

Restoration of Order in Ireland

In the 1918 General Election, Sinn Féin decimated the once proud Irish Parliamentary Party.

On 21 January 1919, it called a meeting at the Mansion House in Dublin of a new Irish parliament called Dáil Éireann. The Dáil called on the world to recognise it as the legitimate Government of Ireland. By coincidence another meeting had been held in the Mansion House earlier that day. The meeting was of 400 Royal Dublin Fusiliers who had been held as prisoners of war during the Great War. According to one press report 'some good-natured bantering passed between soldiers and civilians, while many sympathisers found themselves accidentally mixed up in a Sinn Féin gathering, as they cheered and waved handkerchiefs to the men striding proudly by flourishing miniature flags of the allied nations.' [1]

Far from this scene a consignment of 150 lbs of gelignite was being transported under police escort from Tipperary town to a nearby quarry at Soloheadbeg. The escort was ambushed by a group of Irish Volunteers that included Dan Breen, Sean Hogan, Seamus Robinson and Sean Treacy. During the encounter two policemen guarding the consignment were killed. They were Constable McDonnell from Belmullet, County Mayo, a 50-year-old widower, and Constable O'Connell, from Coachford, County Cork, who was 30 years old and had been planning to be married in a couple of months. Instead of fleeing the country as so many had done before them 'the big four', as they came to be known, went on the run. In response to the attack at Soloheadbeg the Government declared Tipperary a Martial Law area. The first steps had been taken in the War of Independence.

During 1919 the conflict was limited in its scope. Small groups of Irish Volunteers attacked Royal Irish Constabulary (RIC) barracks, banks, post offices and tax offices. In December an assassination attempt was made on the Viceroy, Lord French. However, it was still a low-key conflict. During the entire year eighteen policemen and one soldier were killed. In 1920 the scale of the conflict grew considerably. Although Dáil Éireann had been suppressed in September 1919, Sinn Féin won control of eleven of twelve cities and boroughs in Ireland. The Irish Volunteers became known as the Irish Republican Army and increased its military effort. While areas of the countryside were given over to the IRA, a curfew was imposed in Dublin from midnight until 5 a.m. The Irish administration based in Dublin Castle, that had ruled the country so effectively for decades, proved itself incapable of coping with the developing situation. Sinn Féin's Arthur Griffith claimed that from January 1919 to the summer of 1920 Crown forces had carried out 38,720 raids on private houses, arrested nearly 5,000 people and Crown forces had made 1,604 armed assaults against the Irish population.[2] Reprisals by police against the civilian population were commonplace. However, there was little to show for all this action except an increasingly hostile public. In the spring there was a change of personnel at Dublin Castle. Sir Hamar Greenwood, a Conservative politician who was born in Canada, was appointed Chief Secretary. Henry Tudor was put in charge of the police in Ireland while Sir Nevile Macready was made Commander-in-Chief of the Army in Ireland.

One of the main issues that the new administration needed to address was the condition of the police in Ireland. Resignations had haemorrhaged the force and to make up for those who had left recruits were brought over from England. These recruits became known as the Black and Tans. In May 1920, Bonar Law reported to Prime Minister Lloyd George that at a meeting on the Irish situation a 'suggestion was made with favour by everyone which I think you and I discussed before - that a special body of Ex-Service men here in England should be enlisted on special terms as gendarmerie to be used in Ireland and the War Office are to prepare a scheme as to how they would propose to carry this out.'[3] At the end of July 1920 this force, known as the Auxiliaries and under the command of Brigadier General Crozier, arrived in Ireland to patrol disturbed areas.

While the British were bolstering their forces in Ireland (ultimately there would be 50,000 police and military in Ireland) *An T-Oglaigh*, the IRA publication, published the following article.

An T-Oglaigh Vol. II. No. 12. 1 June 1920

A FATEFUL TIME

The present time is certain to be a fateful one in Ireland's history, and on the discipline, courage and efficiency of the Irish Republican Army will largely depend the issue of the combat. The enemy at the present moment is pouring men, equipment and munitions of war into this country. His plan of campaign has not yet developed but the inspired forecasts in enemy papers (whether deliberately published with intent or not) indicate an intention of acting chiefly on the defensive. Whether this will be the line of action of the enemy army or not largely depends on ourselves. His intention may really be to strengthen his forces solely with a view to defensive, or at most to counter-offensive, action; but it is quite certain, that if we remain inactive, the enemy will not long remain so, and a violent offensive against us may be anticipated.

We pointed out in these columns some months ago that the offensive had passed from the enemy's hands to ours and that it was our business to retain the advantage we had gained; that it was our duty to make our guerrilla warfare against the enemy still more intense and menacing; to give his forces not a moment's ease or rest in any part of the country. This line of action has been followed out to a considerable extent, though not in as widespread a manner as it should, it still remains our object. Since we wrote, large tracts of country have been abandoned by the enemy forces, and the abandoned barracks and other strongholds have been destroyed by our troops. In most of those places Republican law is now predominant and peace and order is successfully maintained by the Volunteers. Had all the Brigades been equally efficient and equally active, the enemy's hold on the country today would be even more precarious than it is.

To keep up the fight effectively it is necessary that every officer, every corps, and every individual Volunteer should maintain themselves at the highest point of efficiency. Prompt and cheerful obedience to orders, and zeal, skill and courage in carrying them out on the part of all will bring us far. In recent operations throughout the country the number of mishaps or miscarriages was exceedingly small. The men who were able to do so much successfully should be able to bring off much bigger things, if they keep themselves 'on tap' and leave no stone unturned to perfect their organisation, training, and equipment. It will be necessary for us all to strain every nerve to intensify the warfare against the invader and make his position an impossible one. In some parts of the country opportunities are being neglected at the present time which may not be there at a later date, and Volunteers may be lamenting lost chances when it is too late.

In the summer of 1920, the British administration had come to the conclusion that there existed in large parts of Ireland a state of complete disorder and lawlessness. Most serious was the fact that policemen and soldiers were being killed with near impunity. It was not only very difficult to catch those who carried out such acts but those who were charged were let go by civilian courts. In the House of Commons a frustrated Lloyd George reported that in the month of July alone 15 police and 4 military had been killed and 52 wounded.[4] Over 50 policemen had been killed since the beginning of the year but no one had been convicted for their deaths.[5] Countering such figures Sinn Féin stated that 31 civilians had been killed by Government forces.[6] In the view of the Government the ordinary law on the statute books, which was already supplemented by the Defence of the Realm Act brought in during World War One, was deemed 'inadequate for the prevention and punishment of crime or the maintenance of order'.[7] Some of the hardliners in the Cabinet argued that the only way to deal with rebelliousness in Ireland was the imposition of strict and brutal martial law that would confer on the military draconian powers (counties in the south-west had already been declared military areas but were run jointly between the civil administration and the military). However, the majority of the British Cabinet was reluctant to sanction such a course. To address the situation in Ireland the Restoration of Order in Ireland Bill (ROI) was rushed through the parliament in Westminster in early August 1920.

One of the few dissenting voices was one of the last remaining members of the Irish Parliamentary Party, Paddy Devlin, MP for Belfast. During the debate Devlin asked Lloyd George if he was 'aware that the policy of the Government is driving moderate men of all sections into the extreme movement. Is the policy of the Government not to leave a single leg for a moderate man to stand on in Ireland?'[8] The ROI Bill provided for a host of rules and regulations including prohibition on the possession of carrier pigeons, prohibition on the use of secret means of communication, power to close pubs early, power to search and question, power to require inhabitants to remain indoors, and power to take possession of and fell trees. One of the most controversial aspects of the Bill was that a death caused by Crown forces would no longer be subject to a coroner's inquest but to an army inquest. In the supplemental regulations a section dealt with the trial and punishment of crimes by court martial. These court martials were aimed at overcoming the difficulty that existed in securing convictions in the civilian courts. In these court martials each person being tried was treated as if he belonged to the military unit in whose charge he was being held. The jury in these court martials consisted of British military officers (the names of Irish officers or of officers whose homes were in Ireland would not be submitted for these juries). In an attempt to try to ensure fairness, each court would have appointed to it a person of legal knowledge and experience. This person would be nominated by the Lord Lieutenant and certified by the Lord Chancellor of Ireland or the Lord Chief Justice of England. When the Bill was introduced in Westminster one English MP, Mr Bottomley, said, 'I can conceive of no step more calculated to outrage and inflame Irish opinion than the introduction of this military system which is utterly unnecessary… I know something of the system of court martial, and I do not adopt the Chief Secretary's eulogium of its equity or of the care with which the tribunals are conducted.'[9]

From October 1920 to June 1921, over two-dozen people were tried by these court martials. Ten were sentenced to death and hanged for Ireland.[10]

> *1 November 1920* – *Kevin Barry*
> *14 March 1921* – *Patrick Moran*
> *14 March 1921* – *Thomas Whelan*
> *14 March 1921* – *Thomas Bryan*
> *14 March 1921* – *Patrick Doyle*
> *14 March 1921* – *Frank Flood*
> *14 March 1921* – *Bernard Ryan*
> *25 April 1921* – *Thomas Traynor*
> *7 June 1921* – *Edmund Foley*
> *7 June 1921* – *Patrick Maher*

The ten were buried in Mountjoy prison and their remains stayed there for over 80 years. In October 2001, the ten bodies were disinterred. Nine were reburied in Glasnevin cemetery while one, Patrick Maher, was reburied in Ballylanders, Co. Limerick. Before this event the only name that would have held any degree of familiarity for most people was that of Kevin Barry. However, the British authorities thought that these ten men had committed crimes serious enough to warrant their executions. Presumably it was thought that these executions would serve some purpose during the War of Independence. However, the executions were another example of British policy that exacerbated relations with Ireland, without going far enough to meet their own ends. The executions did not shorten the period of insurrection in Ireland, they did not act as an appreciable deterrent to others. If anything, the executions gave more impetus to the nationalist movement. For many the executions of the ten became ten more reasons to end British rule in Ireland.

Executions

In April 1866, John Logue was hanged outside Downpatrick Gaol. He was the last person publicly executed in Ireland. After that all executions were brought in behind the closed doors and high walls of prisons. One reason for the ending of public executions was the belief that it would be more dignified for the 'culprit' to be executed in private. Another reason was that executions were often 'messy' with the unfortunate person being strangled to death instead of dying instantaneously as was intended. With the ending of public executions the authorities attempted to regulate them to allay public fears of unnecessary cruelty. A 'Table of Drops' detailed the length of rope that should be used to ensure the quick death of the victim, rather than slow strangulation, without the drop being so long as to outwardly mutilate the victim. As part of the regulation of executions instructions were issued detailing procedure throughout.

FORM 80C. 157.

A.D

Confidential.

(By order of the Lord Lieutenant this document is to be treated as most strictly confidential, and, in any case, when a copy is supplied to a Sheriff he is requested to return it to the Prison Governor from whom he received it.)

MEMORANDUM OF INSTRUCTIONS FOR CARRYING OUT THE DETAILS OF AN EXECUTION.

1. The apparatus for the execution may be tested in the following manner:
   The working of the scaffold should be first tested without any weight. Then a

bag of sand of the same weight as the culprit should be attached to the rope, and so adjusted as to allow the bag a drop equal to or rather more than that which the culprit shall receive, so that the rope may be stretched with a force of about 900 foot pounds. The working of the apparatus under these conditions should then be tested. The bag must be of the approved pattern, with a thick and well padded neck, so as to prevent any injury to the rope and leather.

2. After the completion of this testing the scaffold and all appliances should be locked up, and kept by the Governor or other responsible officer until the morning of the execution; but the bag of sand should remain suspended all the night preceding the execution, so as to take the stretch out of the rope.

3. The Executioner and any persons appointed to assist in the operation should make themselves thoroughly acquainted with the working of the apparatus.

4. The lever should be fixed so as to prevent any accident while the preliminary details are being carried out.

5. Death by hanging ought to result from dislocation of the neck. The length of the drop is determined according to the weight of the culprit.

6. The required length of drop is regulated as follows:
At the end of the rope which forms the noose the Executioner should see that 13 inches from the centre of the ring are marked off by a line painted round the rope; this is to be a fixed quantity, which, with the stretching of this portion of the rope and the lengthening of the neck and body of the culprit will represent the average depth of the head and circumference of the neck after constriction. About two hours before the execution the bag of sand should be raised out of the pit and be allowed another drop so as to completely stretch the rope. Then while the bag of sand is still suspended the Executioner should measure off from the painted line on the rope the required length of drop, and should make a chalk mark on the rope at the end of the length. A piece of copper wire fastened to the chain should now be stretched down the rope till it reaches the chalk mark, and should be cut off there so that the cut end of the copper wire shall terminate at the upper end of the measured length of drop. The bag of sand should be then raised from the pit and disconnected from the rope. The chain should now be so adjusted at the bracket that the lower end of the copper wire shall reach to the same level from the floor of the scaffold as the height of the prisoner. The known height

of the prisoner can be readily measured on the scaffold by a graduated rule of six feet long. When the chain has been raised to the proper height the cotter must be securely fixed through the bracket and chain. The Executioner should now make a chalk mark on the floor of the scaffold in a plumb line with the chain, where the prisoner should stand.

These details should be carried out as soon as possible after six o'clock [executions were normally scheduled for 8 a.m.] so as to allow the rope time to regain a portion of its elasticity before the execution.

7. The copper wire should now be detached, and after allowing sufficient amount of rope for the easy adjustment of the noose, the slack of the rope should be fastened to the chain above the level of the head of the culprit with a pack-thread. The pack-thread should be just strong enough to support the rope without breaking.

8. When all the preparations are completed the scaffold should remain in charge of a responsible officer while the Executioner goes to the pinioning room.

9. The pinioning apparatus should be dextrously applied in some room or place convenient to the scaffold. When the culprit is pinioned and his neck is bared he should be at once conducted to the scaffold.

10. On reaching the gallows, the duty of The Executioner should be as follows:-
    (1) Place the culprit *exactly* under the part of the beam to which the rope is attached.
    (2) Strap the culprit's legs tightly.
    (3) Put on the white linen cap.
    (4) Put on the rope around the neck quite tightly (with the cap between the rope and the neck), the metal eye being directed forwards, and placed in front of the angle of the lower jaw, so that with the constriction of the neck it may come underneath the chin. The noose should be kept tight by means of a stiff leather washer, or an india-rubber washer, or a wedge.
    (5) Go *quickly* to the lever and let down the trap-doors.

11. The culprit should hang one hour, and then the body should be *carefully* raised from the pit. The rope should be removed from the neck, and also the straps from the body. In laying out the body for the inquest, the head should be raised three inches by placing a small piece of wood under it.[11]

Notes to the text

1. *Irish Times*, 22 January 1919.

2. *Irish Bulletin*, Vol. 2, No. 66, 5 August 1920.

3. House of Lords, Lloyd George Papers, F31/1/30.

4. Hansard's Debates of the House of Commons, July 19 – August 16, 1920, p. 1971.

5. Ibid. p. 613.

6. *Irish Bulletin*, Vol. 2, No. 66, 5 August 1920.

7. Report of the Committee appointed to review the provisions of the Restoration of Order in Ireland Act, 1920, and of the Regulations made under that Act, HMSO, 1924, p. 4.

8. *Irish Times*, 3 August 1920.

9. Hansard's Debates of the House of Commons, July 19 – August 16, 1920, p. 2803.

10. These were not the only people executed by the British during the War of Independence. There were 14 executed in Limerick and Cork. Because they were in a martial law area they were not hanged but were executed by firing squad. Some were executed just 24 hours after their capture.

11. Public Record Office, Prison Commission, 8/212.

1

Kevin Barry

Attack on military ration escort at North King Street, Dublin, 20 September 1920

On 1 November 1920, at eight o'clock, Kevin Barry was hanged in Mountjoy Prison's hanghouse. That afternoon he was buried in the grounds of the prison. No family members or other 'outsiders' were allowed to attend the funeral. Canon Waters, the prison's chaplain for over twenty years, later described to Mrs Barry the funeral of her son.

> The grave appeared to me to be about 3½ feet deep. There we laid all that was mortal of poor Kevin in blessed clay and with all Catholic prayer and rites. The warders covered in the grave and we said the *De Profundis*. Some half-dozen soldiers who came to the door of the barracks close by, and some matrons who were looking on from a neighbouring window, were the only spectators. It was a sad funeral indeed but I hope to live to see him removed from this and to receive from his countrymen the honours due to his heroic virtues.[1]

Over half a million prisoners have passed through the doors of Mountjoy Prison. Among them have been many distinguished historical figures, Jeremiah O'Donovan Rossa, Eamon de Valera, Sean MacBride, Countess Markievicz and Brendan Behan to name but a few. However, no name is more associated with 'the Joy' than that of Kevin Barry. For generations the name Kevin Barry has been part of Ireland's national consciousness. This is partly due to the ballad, *Kevin Barry*, written in his honour – for most people the sum total of what they know is found in the words of this ballad. However, the execution of Kevin Barry had a significance far beyond the words of a ballad. He was the first of ten men hanged in Mountjoy Prison during the War of Independence. He was also the first political prisoner executed in Ireland since the leaders of the 1916 Rising were shot in Kilmainham Gaol. Barry's execution was all the more poignant because of his age, he was just 18 years old, and because of statements made about his treatment during questioning. The execution of Barry was also significant in the wider context of the War of Independence. Author, historian and journalist Tim Pat Coogan has called the case of Barry one of the 'moral turning points' of the War of Independence.[2] It was a defining moment in an increasingly bitter conflict between the independence movement and the British Crown.

Kevin Barry was born at 8 Fleet Street, Dublin on 20 January 1902. The middle child of seven children, his parents ran a dairy business. Barry's father died when he was just six. Most of the family then moved to Tombeagh, Hacketstown, Co. Carlow. When Kevin was 15 he returned to Dublin. He first went to O'Connells School on the North Circular Road, then St. Mary's, Rathmines and afterwards to Belvedere College where he played hurling and rugby. Described as a very bright student Barry went on to study medicine in UCD. A seemingly promising career lay ahead. However, political events soon overtook the medical student.

Kevin Barry.

Kevin Barry was first introduced to the independence movement at a Manchester Martyr Commemoration Concert in the Mansion House. Following the meeting Barry wanted to join the Volunteer's boy scouts, Fianna Éireann. However, it was the death in Mountjoy of Thomas Ashe from force-feeding while on hunger strike, in October 1917, that finally led him to take action. At the age of 15 he joined Auxiliary C Company of the First Battalion, Dublin Brigade of the Irish Volunteers. During the War of Independence Barry became an active member. On 1 June 1920 he took part in a raid for arms on the King's Inn. Barry was one of the first into the building. A comrade later recalled, 'I have a picture in my mind of Kevin Barry coming out of the guardroom with a Lewis gun hugged in his arms. His boyish face was wreathed in smiles, as he said to me, "Look, Dinny, what I have got!" I could not help laughing, even in the excitement of the moment, and thinking that he looked like a child clasping a new toy to his chest.' [3] In July, while spending the summer in Carlow, he was attached to the Third Battalion of the Carlow Brigade. Among other actions, he was involved in the burning of Hacketstown Barracks, one of the first to be burned in a concerted IRA campaign to drive the RIC out of rural areas.[4] During the summer he wrote the following carefree letters to a student friend Jack Lynch.

Tombeagh

Hacketstown

Co Carlow

21/7/20

Dear Jack

I don't know how to apologise for not writing sooner but I am a rotten correspondent. Well anyway, how the divil are you? I hope you are not affected by the trouble these Sinn Feiners are causing.

There is no news of any interest here. I had a letter from Vincent sometime ago – he was making hay. I had several letters from Jerry the last from Lough Derg, but I had no word from McLaughlin. Neither had Jerry.

I came home here about three weeks ago, got fed up and returned to town. I had a hell of a great fortnight. Stopped with another fellow all the time and was drunk every night with the result that I'm back here a nervous wreck.

I met Paddy Nugent several times at the Empire. By the way are you still backing horses. I've given it up since yesterday. I backed Cooldrinagh at the Curragh. Straight tip – 3rd at evens.

Now I'll have to shut up. Hoping you are enjoying yourself.

Yours till hell freezes

K.G.B. [5]

Tombeagh
Hacketstown
8:ix:20

Dear John

You are indeed an awful pup. I had cut you out of my will and had erased your name from the vast recesses of my memory, so that I was quiet annoyed at getting a letter from you.

Now as for that bastard Shields – that fellow is a low tout. His language is redolent of the law courts and his mind is a sink of iniquity. As to the joke you refer to, I can assure you I am entirely innocent and can only conclude that the whole thing is a fabrication of his low legal imagination.

I was up in town for a few days about 3 weeks ago. The place was deserted and Mick Mullins and John O'Donnell were the only surviving college men to be seen. I am going up next Sat as you are doubtless unaware that I have an exam this day week and I know... all.

And now Jack a word of advice chuck horses but don't forget to back Rocklow for the Dalkey Donkey Derby.

Now au revoir and answer this soon. By the way, McLaughlin writes me every week. Joe and he are on the run at present.

Yours till I'm qualified

Kevin. [6]

Barry was back in Dublin in September to resit his failed first year exams. On 20 September he was scheduled to sit his last one. However, that morning he had another appointment. It was an ambush at 11 o'clock at the junction of Church Street and North King Street on the north side of Dublin. Today it is a busy junction which shows little evidence of the narrow shop-lined streets that were there at the time of the attack. The only indication of a connection with that morning is the name Kevin Barry on the overlooking local authority flats. The target for the ambush that September morning was a military escort guarding bread which was being collected from Monk's bakery on Church Street to provision the military camp at Collinstown (now Dublin airport). The purpose of the raid was the capture of the arms of the military escort. Barry thought it would be over well in time for his afternoon exam. During the attack, in which he took a leading role, his gun jammed (having left his own gun in Carlow he was issued with another one from his quartermaster that morning). While he was trying to free the mechanism his comrades retreated from the scene. Barry was left isolated and sought cover under the military lorry. He was discovered, captured, and put into the back of the lorry under the guard of the military. Also put into the back of the lorry were three dead or mortally wounded soldiers. The next day the *Freeman's Journal* reported on the attack.

Freeman's Journal, 21 September 1920

FIERCE AFFRAY IN DUBLIN

ARMED CIVILIANS MAKE DARING ATTACK ON ARMED MILITARY. TWO SOLDIERS KILLED.

Terrifying Scenes in Busy Thoroughfare; Wounded Civilian Captured

A busy Dublin thoroughfare was the scene of a sensational occurrence during the busy hours of yesterday morning.

While a military lorry with armed soldiers was waiting for bread supplies from a bakery, armed civilians came up and entered into conflict with the soldiers. Rifles and revolvers were used. While the encounter was proceeding outside shots were also fired in the yard of the bakery. Passers-by were onlookers on the desperate affair and saw casualties on both sides. Two soldiers were killed and three were wounded, one seriously. The fight, for such it was, lasted but a couple of minutes. Prior to it some armed civilians entered the bakery and went out to the yard, where the telephone connection was cut.

Civilians Attend The Wounded

A fierce encounter between soldiers and armed civilians in a Dublin City thoroughfare. One soldier was killed, another died from wounds, another was dangerously wounded, and two were slightly wounded. It is also believed one civilian was wounded and taken prisoner.

The scene of the desperate affair was Church Street, abutting North King Street, and in and about the bakery establishment of Messrs P. Monks and Co. A military lorry with armed soldiers of the Duke of Wellington Regiment had arrived from Collinstown Barracks, some time after 11 o'clock, to take away the bread supply for those barracks for which Messrs Monks and Co. are contractors.

It was drawn up at the entrance to the yard of the bakery. In it were some nine or ten soldiers, while others were in the yard, having been detailed for the removal of the bread from the stores.

Rifles and Revolvers

From what could be ascertained, about a dozen young men had sauntered up North King Street about 11 o'clock, and, dividing into two, one batch entered the premises of Messrs Monks and passed through to the yard, the other, numbering also five or six, passed into Church Street and walked slowly up the right-hand side of the thoroughfare, some reading newspapers.

An eye-witness told the Freeman representative he saw one of these latter move suddenly into the middle of the road, and, presenting a revolver at the soldiers in the lorry, shouted 'Hands up!'. In a moment the air resounded with the sounds of rifle and revolver fire.

Others state the firing was preceded by a loud explosion, as if a bomb or a hand-grenade had been used, but no trace of any such weapon could be found afterwards. At all events, the alarmed onlookers and terror-stricken passers-by saw one of the soldiers on the lorry drop within the vehicle, and a moment later, one of the civilians dropped on the street close to the lorry, rolling beneath it, apparently wounded. He was afterwards captured and taken off to the barracks at the North Dublin Union, which is about a quarter of a mile away. On him were found a revolver and some ammunition. His companions had disappeared down the street.

The remains of the soldiers killed in the attack at King Street were transported to England during the following week. A large body of troops escorted the coffins containing Privates Washington, Humphries and Whitehead, all members of the Duke of Wellington's (West Riding Regiment), to a steamer at Dublin Port. Four military bands marched in the procession and respectful crowds lined the route.[7]

Church Street after the attack on the military.

On 20 October, Barry was brought under strong military escort from Mountjoy Prison to his court martial in Marlborough Barracks (now McKee Barracks). The barracks was chosen on the grounds of security and because of its proximity to Mountjoy Prison. At precisely 10 a.m., the members of the court martial took their places. Barry's mother and sister gave moral support as the judicial drama was played out in front of their eyes. Barry was charged under the Restoration of Order (Ireland) Act with feloniously wounding and killing Private Matthew Whitehead. This was the first case in which a person was tried for a capital crime under the new regulations. Kevin Barry told the court that as a soldier of the Irish Republic he regarded all of his actions as acts of war. As a soldier of Ireland he refused to recognise the court and did not put forward a defence.

In his opening address the Prosecutor outlined the evidence against the medical student.

Prosecutor Addresses the Court: *[Underlining as in the original manuscript]*

> May it please the Court, the charge against this young man who is before the Court, is one of the gravest possible character – a charge of murder, and to me has been allotted the degree of presenting the case to the Court. I trust that I shall be able to do so in a temperate and perfectly fair manner, especially having regard to the fact that his interests are not guarded professionally in this case by anyone except myself, who's duty it is to see that these interests are fully respected. This is, I understand, the first case of this kind which has had to be tried by such a tribunal as is sitting here to-day, rendered unfortunately necessary by the somewhat disturbed conditions through which we are passing. I take no part, I take no interest in politics; I am here as Prosecuting Counsel, and as a minister of justice, to endeavour to help the court to come to the right conclusion upon the evidence, and not to influence their minds, or to endeavour to prejudice them by any political considerations at all. The facts are quite simple: On the morning of the 20th September, a Monday, a ration lorry was dispatched from Collinstown Camp to draw bread from Monk's bakery which is in Church Street. Sergt. Banks, was in charge of that lorry. It contained the driver, a private in the Royal Army Service Corps; two unarmed men who were to act as fatigue to obtain the bread from the bakery and convey it to the lorry, and six armed men whose names were Privates Washington, <u>Whitehead</u>, Humphries, Dalby, Newton and Cleary. The two unarmed men were Smith and Noble; the one unarmed driver was Private Barnes...

> A little after 11 o'clock in the morning a lorry arrived at the bakery, and there stopped just beyond the passage leading into the bakery, on the right-hand side of Church Street, going north... The lorry, passing through Church Street, had arrived just beyond the entrance to Monk's bakery, on the right-hand side, going north, and as it

arrived Sergt. Banks and one of the armed men, Humphries, sitting with the driver – the other seven men, that is, five armed and two fatigue men were in the back of the lorry; on arrival... Sergt. Banks got down and entered the passage leading into Monk's bakery... that leads in from the street in to the bakery yard, and he went in there to see if the bread for which the party had come was ready for delivery. Private Noble, one of the unarmed men, let down the tail-board of the lorry, and he and Private Smith – the other unarmed man – got out. Banks then, having ascertained inside the bakery that the bread was ready for them, returned again to fetch the fatigue men, and led the way back into the yard with the two men, Noble and Smith, following him. Whilst passing through the passage Sergt. Banks heard shots fired into the street, he says he thinks about ten shots were fired; looking ahead of him he saw a man standing at the right-hand corner of the passage, facing him... This man fired two shots, neither of them hit Sergt. Banks who pursued his course into the manager's office which is round to the left as he got into the bakery yard. But when Sergt. Banks got through to the manager's office he was confronted immediately by a man with a pistol in his hand, who pointed it at him... Banks struck at him with his fists, and this armed man struck back with the pistol in his hand, and hit Sergt. Banks with it on the head... Sergt. Banks was closely followed up the passage by Noble and Smith, and before any shot was fired they heard a cry from the street behind them – Noble describes it as a cry of 'Hands up', Smith as 'Hands up', both heard the cry of 'Hands up', Noble, looking round behind him, saw three civilians pointing pistols at the lorry, he also saw, as he would say, four or five other civilians with pistols in their hands in the bakery yard...The men who were in the yard fired down, or one man fired down the passage, and firing started in the street, and as soon as the firing commenced Noble, who was one of the fatigue men, was hit by a shot from the yard or from the street, he cannot say which; he was hit by a shot in the left ankle, in consequence of that he fell down. Smith was close to him at the time

Noble was hit. Smith thinks he saw more men than Noble saw on the street at that time, he saw them firing in the direction of the lorry; he saw men in the passage between him and the court-yard, firing in his direction, he was at that time a yard or two down the passage, he was struck by a bullet in the right elbow, but he stayed with Noble who by that time had fallen and was beside him.

Marlborough Barracks, Dublin.

Barnes was the driver of the lorry, and before any firing occurred he got down from his seat to see to his engine, and whilst so engaged... a man came towards the lorry and fired a pistol <u>in the air</u>; I presume he came towards the front of the lorry from the direction of New Brunswick Street. A number of shots were then fired, and they rang out from the direction behind the lorry, and the direction of the bakery yard. Barnes got on to the driver's seat, and then he saw Humphries, who had been sitting on the box-sent by his side, was wounded and bleeding from a wound in the abdomen. Private Dalby, one of the armed guard, saw four men approach the lorry from the rear, <u>and one of these men was the prisoner —the accused</u>. There were four of them, one of them was the accused and they were <u>wearing rain-proofcoats</u> at the time they came up to the lorry. They drew their pistols and shouted 'Hands up' and 'Hand over your arms', and without waiting further they fired. <u>The accused had in his hand a pistol, he was seen to fire it into the lorry in the direction of one of the soldiers in the lorry, and who immediately fell. That man was shot through the chin.</u>

That was not the man Whitehead, whose death we are considering the responsibility for in this case. The firing having commenced, <u>the accused having taken part in it,</u> the guard opened fire, and one of the attacking party was hit. The attacking party was then joined by the two or three men who had been up in the bakery yard, together they took their wounded comrade away up the street. That was all that Dalby saw of the occurrence. Cleary was another armed guard, and he saw five men approaching the lorry from the rear, with rain coats on, they shouted '<u>Hands up</u>' and 'hand over your rifles', exactly the same cry that Dalby had heard; these men opened fire with the automatic pistols with which they were armed, <u>he too would identify the accused as one of the men, and he saw him actually firing just before Private Washington fell.</u> The men then, having started firing their pistols, and the guard having opened fire, they ran back, says Cleary, in the direction from which they came, that is south; he cannot say if they all ran back, but some of them ran back, he does not know whether they all did. Barnes, the driver, then went into the bakery yard to fetch out the sergeant in charge of the party; he came out, he gave Barnes, the driver, an order; Barnes started off his engine and got up into his seat. When the Sergeant came out – he up to that time had been unarmed – he took from Private Cleary the rifle which the man Washington, who was by that time dead in the lorry, had been carrying, and with this rifle in his hand <u>he saw a man lying under the front of the lorry, with his face to the ground, carrying a pistol in his hand;</u> covering him with his rifle he called on him to come out and put up his hands, and the <u>accused came out. He dropped the pistol when he came out,</u> and Banks picked it up and handed it over to the driver, Barnes, and told the accused to get into the lorry, he did so, and there he was effectively guarded. One will wonder, of course, how the accused was under the front of the lorry. It may be that the other attackers, having got away, the accused thought he would more effectively shelter from the danger of flying bullets by getting underneath the lorry, that may have been his object, I do not know, but if Dalby and Cleary are correct in identifying the accused as being the man that they saw with a pistol in his hand, and firing it, it is quite obvious he must have gone there for some purpose which we need not fathom, but which was obvious to himself at that moment.

Noble and Smith were wounded in the entrance to the bakery yard. Two civilians assisted to carry Noble to Richmond Hospital; and Smith, with the assistance of the guard, got there too. The lorry, with the rest of the party, with Humphries wounded in it, with Whitehead wounded in it, as we shall see, and with Washington in it dead, with the accused in safe custody, reached the North Dublin Union... the accused was handed over to the N.C.O. of the guard at the North Dublin Union. That N.C.O. was Sergt. Brain, and to him was also handed by the driver of the lorry a <u>German automatic pistol – the pistol which the accused had dropped when he was told to come out from under the lorry, and there was taken out from it a magazine containing two live cartridges; in the chamber of the pistol, and ready for firing, there was one other cartridge; these three were extracted... The two rounds in the magazine were flat-nosed bullets, the one in the chamber was round-nosed.</u> There is a heterogeneous collection of ammunition, the two flatnosed bullets had nickel casing, and the <u>round-nosed bullet had copper casing; the importance of that will become more clear presently.</u> Lieutenant Deane in due course handed that pistol and ammunition to Capt. Cross, Adjutant, who put it safely in the orderly room. The accused was spoken to by an officer of the Lancashire Fusiliers, and when he was asked why he had attacked the lorry he was heard to make use of this very important phrase: '<u>We were after the rifles</u>.' And the accused said afterwards that he had been ordered by an Officer to take the lorry that morning. It will be quite clear that the accused would wish it to be understood that he does not recognise the authority of the Court, and what he was engaged in then, if an offence at all, was <u>an act of war</u>. It cannot be too clearly pointed out that it is high treason to commit an act of war in the King's realms, and if that be his state of mind, that he was carrying out an act of war, it would be high treason in law. 'We were after the rifles', that, in itself, would be an admission that he was out with others engaged in the commission of a felony; and it cannot be too clearly pointed out that any persons who are engaged in a felonious act, who, in the course of carrying that act out commit or cause the death of a person, that is <u>murder</u>, and it matters not whether his be the hand that pressed the trigger and caused the death; if one person was engaged to commit such an act in furtherance of the common design of the party, his act is the act of all, and all are equally responsible in law for the consequences. Private Whitehead was taken from the lorry wounded, he was in an extremely serious condition, and all that medical skill could do was brought to bear to save his life; thereby, possibly, to save the accused from meeting the charge which he now has to meet. Lieut. Colonel Palmer was at King George V Hospital when Whitehead was brought in. He was taken from the North Dublin Union to King George V Hospital. He was wounded in the <u>left side of the abdomen</u> by a bullet, and it was obvious that this <u>bullet was lodged in his body</u> because there was no wound of exit. He was operated upon by Sir William Taylor, the then Consulting Surgeon of Forces in Ireland, every possible step was taken to save his life. The attendant cut away his clothing for the purpose of the operation which was necessary. There were found four perforations in the bowel, these were sewn up and some bleeding vessels were ligatured. The cavity of the abdomen was found to be full of clotted blood and fluid, and that was cleared with the flat of the hand, and it was in that way that the bullet, <u>which was then lying in the body, was taken from the body;</u> it was not, at that moment, observed, but that is the only way in which it can have been removed from the body of Whitehead. He was transferred to the wards, and <u>died fifteen minutes afterwards</u> as a result of this wound.

Before the operating theatre had time to be cleared out his place was taken on the operating table by Humphries who was in a similar condition. In the case of Humphries the bullet had made its mark of entrance, but there was also a mark of exit, so that the bullet which caused his wound would not be likely to be found in his body. He was operated upon, but he died about fifteen or twenty minutes afterwards. The hospital attendant then set about clearing up the operating theatre; the place was covered with swabs and blood, and when he was clearing the operating table, sweeping it on to the floor, <u>he touched something heavy which turned out to be a bullet. That bullet will be produced for you to see. It is a bullet of the same calibre and the same character as that which was found in the pistol which the accused was carrying;</u> it is a bullet which had been fired through <u>a pistol of the same pattern,</u> for it has upon it the marks of six grooves corresponding exactly with the grooves in the barrel of the pistol which the accused possessed, and <u>it will be obvious that it was that which caused the death of Whitehead.</u>

It was obvious from an examination of the pistol which the accused was carrying that it had been fired, probably that morning, for there was <u>superficial fouling upon it,</u> and it was obvious that the superficial fouling had been caused about that time. It will be proved to you that that is the bullet which was picked up in that operating theatre following the operation upon these two men. These are the facts, and it does not require that I should give the Court any lecture upon law; it would be quite sufficient for me, if I am permitted to speak under the Direction of the learned Deputy Judge Advocate, to point out that if several persons are present together, prepared to pursue a common and lawful object at all hazards, and one of them, in furtherance of the original object, commits a criminal act, all are guilty of that act, and for that there is ample authority, but in this case it will be almost proved to demonstration that it was the accused who actually shot the man whose death we are enquiring about now, Private Whitehead.[8]

During the trial witness after witness was called to give their version of the morning's events. Each time Barry was asked if he wanted to question the witness. Each time he replied 'No', except for once when he snapped at the President of the Court, 'Don't bother asking me that question any more, I am not interested in the proceedings.' At times during the trial Barry cheekily showed his disdain and contempt by reading a newspaper as his fate was being decided around him.

If Barry had had a defence counsel, a number of points might have been raised which could have undermined the case of the prosecution. There were no independent witnesses produced to say that Barry fired into the lorry. The only witnesses called were members of the military. According to these witnesses the only person they say they saw Barry shoot was not Private Whitehead whose death he was being tried for. The court assumed that the bullet found on the floor of the operating theatre was the bullet that killed Private Whitehead. This may not have been the case. It was also assumed that Barry must have fired the bullet, but it could have been fired by any of the attackers with another weapon handed out by the quartermaster that morning. Nevertheless it is difficult to see how he could have been found innocent in the circumstances. According to the laws under which he was tried it was not necessary for the prosecution to prove that Barry had fired a fatal shot. It was merely necessary for them to prove that he was part of the attacking party. When the Judge Advocate was summing up, he said that although the specific charge was that Barry 'feloniously, wilfully and of his malice aforethought did kill and murder No. 4603629 Private Matthew Whitehead', it would be sufficient to prove that Whitehead was killed while a felony, in which the accused took part, was being committed. That Barry was part of the group there was little doubt. Despite the curious claims by the prosecutor in his opening address that he was also representing Barry's interests, without a defence counsel the outcome of Barry's trial was a foregone conclusion.

It was a week before Barry was informed of his death sentence. During that time discussions took place about his case at the very highest levels of the British establishment, and included the Prime Minister Lloyd George. However, while Barry was awaiting confirmation of his sentence events in a prison in England were occupying most minds.

On 16 August 1920, Terence MacSwiney, the Lord Mayor of Cork, was tried by court martial on four charges including the possession of a numerical cipher of the type used by the RIC, as well as documents the publication of which 'would be likely to cause disaffection to his Majesty'. He was sentenced to two years imprisonment. MacSwiney served early notice of his intent when he addressed the court, 'I simply say that I have decided the terms of my detention whatever your government may do. I shall be free, alive, or dead, within a month.' MacSwiney immediately commenced a hunger strike. It was to last 73 days. Daily reports emanated from Brixton prison where he was held. There was huge international interest in his case. MacSwiney was determined to die or be released, while the government was equally determined to break the powerful weapon of the hunger strike that had been so effectively used by republicans. MacSwiney died of heart failure on 25 October at 5.30 a.m. Nationalist Ireland went into mourning, the country's newspapers bordered in black.[9] The stories of Barry's impending execution and MacSwiney's funeral shared the headlines in this traumatic week.

On 27 October, Kevin Barry was informed that he would be executed the following Monday, 1 November, unless a reprieve was granted. Barry informed relatives who visited him in prison of his death sentence. Meanwhile, Mountjoy's Governor Munro was sent the following message.

TO: THE GOVERNOR OF MOUNTJOY PRISON DUBLIN.

Whereas KEVIN BERRY, otherwise BARRY, of 58 South Circular Road Dublin now in your custody was by a General Court Martial held at Dublin pursuant to the provisions of the Restoration of Order in Ireland Act 1920 and the Regulations made thereunder convicted of the crime of murder and by a sentence signed on the 20th day of October 1920 sentenced to suffer death by being hanged and whereas I have pursuant to the Warrant granted to me by His Majesty in that belief this day confirmed the said sentence as required by law I hereby order that the said sentence be carried out at Mountjoy Prison, Dublin on the *first* day of *November* at *8 a.m* o'clock by *the executioner to be nominated by me.*

This Order shall be sufficient warrant for the carrying out of the said sentence and I hereby direct you to take all necessary steps for the carrying out of the said sentence in manner aforesaid.

> *Signed at Dublin THIS 27TH DAY OF October 1920.*
> *Gen. Macready*
> *Commanding-in-Chief, the forces in IRELAND.*[10]

The day after receiving notice of his death sentence Barry made a statement in Mountjoy about his treatment during questioning. This treatment quickly became known as the 'torture of Kevin Barry'. It became a central part of the Kevin Barry story. Although brutal, the treatment was mild compared to that meted out to other members of the IRA who had been captured. One reason for this was that Barry was captured by normal British military – he would have fared considerably worse if he had been caught by the Black and Tans or the Auxiliaries. However, the account of his treatment, together with the countdown to his impending execution, heightened emotions.

Barry's Statement

I, Kevin Barry, of 58 South Circular Road, in the County of the City of Dublin, aged 18 years and upwards, solemnly and sincerely declare as follows:

On the 20th., day of September, 1920, I was arrested in Upper Church Street, in the City of Dublin, by a sergeant of the 2nd Duke of Wellington's Regiment, and was brought under escort to the North Dublin Union, now occupied by the military. I was brought into the guardroom and searched. I was then removed to the defaulters' room by an escort with a sergeant-major. The latter and the escort belong to the 1st Lancashire Fusiliers. I was then handcuffed.

About a quarter of an hour after I was placed in the defaulters' room two commissioned officers came in. They both belonged to the 1st Lancashire Fusiliers. They were accompanied by three sergeants of the same unit. A military policeman who had been in the room since I entered it remained. One of the officers asked my name which I gave. He then asked for the names of my companions in the raid or attack. I refused to give them. He tried to persuade me to give the names, and I persisted in refusing. He then sent the sergeant out of the room for a bayonet. When it was brought in the sergeant was ordered by the same officer to point the bayonet at my stomach. The same question as to the names and addresses of my companions were repeated, with the same result. The sergeant was then ordered to turn my face to the wall and point the bayonet to my back. I was so turned. The sergeant then said he would run the bayonet into me if I did not tell. The bayonet was then removed and I was turned round again.

The same officer then said to me that if I persisted in my attitude he would turn me out to the men in the barrack square, and he supposed I knew what that means with the men in their present temper. I said nothing. He ordered the sergeants to put me face down on the floor and twist my arm. I was pushed down on the floor after my handcuffs were removed by the sergeant who went for the bayonet. When I lay on the floor, one of the sergeants knelt on the small of my back, the other two placed one foot each on my back and left shoulder, and the man who knelt on me twisted my right arm, holding it by the wrist with one hand, while he held my hair with the other to pull back my head. The arm was twisted from the elbow joint. This continued, to the best of my judgement, for five minutes. It was very painful. The first officer was standing near my feet, and the officer who accompanied him was still present.

During the twisting of my arm, the first officer continued to question me as to the names and addresses of my companions, and also asked me the name of my company commander and any other officer I knew.

As I still persisted in refusing to answer these questions I was allowed to get up and I was again handcuffed. A civilian came in and repeated the questions, with the same result. He informed me that if I gave all the information I knew I could get off. I was then left in the company of the military policemen; the two officers, the three sergeants and the civilian leaving together.

I could certainly identify the officer who directed the proceedings and put the questions. I am not sure of the others, except the sergeant with the bayonet. My arm was medically treated by an officer of the Royal Army Medical Corps, attached to the North Dublin Union, the following morning, and by the prison hospital orderly afterwards for four or five days.

I was visited by the courtmartial officer last night and he read for me a confirmation of sentence of death by hanging, to be executed on Monday next, and I make this solemn declaration conscientiously believing same to be true and by virtue of the Statutory Declarations Act, 1835.

> *Kevin Gerard Barry*
>
> Declared and subscribed before me at Mountjoy Prison,
> in the County of the City of Dublin, this 28th day of
> October, 1920.
>
> Myles Keogh
> A Justice of the Peace for the said County.[11]

The wheels of execution were set in motion. The day after his court martial the execution chamber at Mountjoy was examined. Some repairs had to be made to it.[12] This was understandable as the only time it had been used was nearly twenty years earlier when the only person previously executed in Mountjoy, John Toole, was hanged for the murder of his partner.[13] The setting of Barry's case was out of the ordinary. The circumstances of the trial were exceptional. Barry was tried in a barracks in front of a military court with members of the British Army for his jury. Barry would be hanged like an ordinary criminal rather than shot like a soldier. Hangman John Ellis began his journey from England. Because of the added danger of carrying out a political execution he had negotiated a rise in his fee.[14] While he readied the hanghouse, tension outside the prison mounted as people grappled with the thought of Barry's execution. In this extract a fellow UCD student wrote of her feelings around the time of Barry's execution.

We had all heard of the affair at North King Street Bakery when a party of auxiliaries were attacked and one of them killed. We knew a medical student had been captured but no one seemed really to believe it as the affair was over and gone a long time before any steps were taken. To our horror we read in the papers one day that Kevin Barry was being tried for 'murder', we read the evidence and the summing up of the prosecutor who mentioned that even if Kevin did not fire the fatal shot the fact that he was levying war was quite sufficient to condemn him... It was ages before the sentence was promulgated but no one was too downhearted until the sentence was known. There were terrible stories current of how the poor fellow was being tortured in Mountjoy to make him reveal the names of his companions. I never experienced anything like the surging fury which the news produced in every one. One night Molloy and I were leaving the Library about 9 o'clock we heard a stop-press being shouted and we interviewed the DMP [Dublin Metropolitan Police] man at the gates. In the latest news was the announcement that Kevin was guilty of murder and sentenced to death, and that the execution would be carried out on 1st November. We were dumbfounded and stunned. The more optimistic hoped for a reprieve on account of his age but many others felt there was no hope for him, he was the first prisoner captured and we felt England would make an example of him to deter others. It was a dreadful fortnight listening to the awful tales of the tortures and sufferings in prison. Everyone was depressed and furiously enraged at the very thought of such cruelty. The whole country wanted a reprieve.[15]

E ach week the British Cabinet's Irish Situation Committee received updates of events in Ireland and set Irish policy. During the last week of October 1920, the main item on the agenda was the death and funeral of Terence MacSwiney. However, Barry's execution did warrant comment. These comments reflected the determination of the Government to carry out the death sentence.

(This Document Is The Property Of His Britannic Majesty's Government.)

Secret   **S.I.C. 51**
Cabinet   **Irish Situation Committees**

Report on the situation in Ireland by the General Officer Commanding-in-Chief, for week ended 30th October, 1920.

General Situation

There is no change in the Military situation. Attacks on lorries conveying troops continue and have increased during the last few days. They are apparently being organised systematically under orders from the Headquarters of the Irish Republican Army. Although local Volunteers no doubt take part in these attacks, it is thought that selected extremists are imported into districts to stiffen up the local men, and the latter are, in the majority of districts, not inclined to initiate these outrages themselves. It is possible that the increase during the last few days represents retaliation for the death of MacSwiney. His sympathisers in Dublin decided to carry out the programme which had been arranged, in spite of the fact that the body was not landed in Dublin. Neither at Cork nor Dublin was there any disorder nor political demonstration, and it was not found necessary to interfere to any appreciable extent with the proceedings. It is evident that the rebel headquarters intended that there should be no excuse for Military interference, probably considering that a decorous ceremony increased the effect of MacSwiney's death for propaganda purposes: it is, however, too early to be sure that some form of organised retaliation will not take place.

The railway situation remains unchanged; the raids for mails on the railways have decreased considerably. A large number of Railway Employees have been dismissed for refusing to operate trains containing troops.

The execution of the man Barry is being extensively exploited by the press for propaganda purposes. It would be a good thing if some person in authority in England would explain publicly that this man was conclusively proved to have shot a soldier with an expanding bullet.[16]

Amid growing concern, numerous attempts were made to change the Government's decision. In the following letter the Archbishop of Dublin writes to the Lord Mayor in an attempt to form a united front.

Archbishop's House
Dublin
29/10/20

My Dear Lord Mayor,

A number of people have been here on different deputations. They saw my Secretary. Their business was to induce me to intercede for the young student who is under sentence of death.

Of course I don't need any deputation to suggest such a course to me. My own view is that it might have a good effect if your Lordship and I made a joint request either to the Lord Lieutenant or to the Chief Secretary whichever is the proper person to apply to.

Perhaps your Lordship when you have thought over this could ring me up at nine in the morning. I expect to be in here, practically all the day.

Not to trouble your Lordship this evening the messenger will not wait for an answer unless told at the Mansion House to do so.

Your Lordships ever faithfully,

William J. Walsh
Archbishop of Dublin.[17]

Mansion House, Dublin.

Meanwhile, sections of the press joined in the chorus of calls for a reprieve. The following article warns of the possible repercussions that the execution could have.

Freeman's Journal, 21 October 1920

THE FATE OF KEVIN BARRY

It is difficult for an Irish paper to deal with the sentence of death which has been passed by court martial on the boy Kevin Barry. To point out what everyone in Ireland knows, that the death of this youth is certain to inflame feeling in Ireland more intensely than anything that has yet happened, will undoubtedly encourage the group responsible for the campaign of repression to strain every nerve to have the execution carried out, in the belief that the storm produced will serve their sinister ends. In spite of the risk we feel that a protest should be made and a warning uttered. Members of the Cabinet have shown a woeful lack of intelligence in the handling of Irish affairs, but even they have admitted that the existing situation is due to English mismanagement. Have they weighed fully their own responsibility for the situation before calling for the death of a boy of eighteen as a blood-sacrifice.

Kevin Barry is to die for taking part in a raid for arms which, whether technically a crime or not, was conducted according to the rules of open war. The attack was made openly, and Barry and his companions did not shirk the risks in matching themselves against better armed opponents. If this does not, in British eyes, wipe out the offence, it ought to procure a commutation of the death sentence, more especially as, in the hundreds of cases where British soldiers have fallen into the hands of Volunteers, they have invariably received courteous and chivalric treatment. Does the British Government lack the nobility to spare one life for the hundreds that have been spared by their opponents?

Politicians of all schools now regard the executions that followed Easter Week as a disastrous blunder, and of those executions the shooting of the boys Heuston and Colbert provoked the deepest resentment. If Kevin Barry shares their fate it will be idle for any statesman to talk of reconciliation to this generation of Irishmen.

The Lord Chancellor of Ireland wrote to the Prime Minister Lloyd George earnestly urging the reprieve of Barry 'on ground of boyhood and that he acted under duress – also because he is the first capital conviction under new procedure… Feeling here for a reprieve universal in all classes as certainly making for better atmosphere…'[18] Arthur Griffith of Sinn Féin issued the following address to the 'Civilised Nations' in which he argued that Barry be given prisoner of war status.

> The boy Kevin Barry whose sworn statement of torture inflicted on him by his captors has been published, has been informed that he is to be hanged on Monday next.
>
> Kevin Barry when captured was one of a body of armed Irish Volunteers which attacked an armed English military escort with the object of disarming them.
>
> Under similar circumstances a body of Irish Volunteers captured on June 1st of the present year a party of 25 English military who were on duty at the Kings Inns, Dublin. [Barry took part in this attack.]

Having disarmed the party the Volunteers immediately released their prisoners.

This was in strict accordance with the conduct of the Volunteers in all such encounters. Hundreds of members of the English armed forces have been from time to time captured by the Volunteers, and in no case was any prisoner maltreated, even though Volunteers had been killed and wounded in the fighting, as in the case of Cloyne, Co. Cork, when after a conflict in which one Volunteer was killed and two wounded, the whole of the opposition forces were captured, disarmed, and set at liberty.

Brigadier-General Lucas of the English Army was taken prisoner by the Irish Volunteers on June 26th this year. During the six weeks of his captivity he was treated in strict accordance with International Law, being afforded all the privileges due to his rank as a prisoner of war.

The English Government now proposes to set aside the high standards maintained by the Irish Volunteers and to execute prisoners of war, previously attempting to brand them before the world as criminals.

Such an outrage upon the law and customs of Nations cannot be permitted to pass in silence by Civilisation. It may be in the power of England to hang an Irish boy of 18 under such circumstances, but it is not in her power to prevent the conscience of mankind reprobating with horror such an action. That conscience Ireland invokes against this intended outrage upon God and man.[19]

At the time Eamon de Valera, President of Sinn Féin, was touring America rallying opinion behind the nationalist cause. The day before Barry's execution he made a speech at New York's Polo Grounds on the tragic events back at home. He finished his speech by quoting from William Butler Yeats' *Cathleen Ni Houlihan* with an almost keening intensity:

> 'MacSwiney and his comrades gave up their lives for their country. The English have killed them. Tomorrow a boy, Kevin Barry, they will hang and, he alike, he will only regret that he has but one life to give. O God!
>
> > *"They shall be remembered forever.*
> > *They shall be alive forever.*
> > *They shall be speaking forever.*
> > *The people shall hear them forever."* [20]

Meanwhile, Barry was writing one of his last letters to his friend Kathleen.

Dear Kathleen,

I have just received your letter and thank you for it from my heart. I've had all sorts of letters during the last few days and I know the ones to be thankful for.

I had quite a busy day today. I had a visit from a most effusive young lady whom I didn't know from Adam. She knew all about me however. She wept, but she meant well. Then I had two sisters of charity, then three more visits, then the chaplain followed by Fr. Albert. I then interviewed two Bon Succour Sisters and finished up with the Chaplain. The boys from the college were up outside the gate and they said the Rosary. They also sang 'The Soldier's Song' which did me more good than you can imagine.

Everybody here is very decent. I have just finished my hallow eve rations of apples and grapes but I missed the nuts. However, there is no rose without a thorn. I want you to thank Eily O'Neill for me for her letter and also for all she has done for mother. And I want you to thank all the people you know who had masses said etc. Of course it is unnecessary to tell you how grateful I am.

I want you to keep up the acquaintance with Jenny and the boys. I believe the usual thing done in my case is to make a speech from the dock or something but I couldn't be serious long enough to do it. Besides anyone who ever knew me would never believe I wrote it.

Now I'll shut up. I wish you every success in love and business. Give my adieux to Des and your mother and say a little prayer when I cash in.

Your pal,

Kevin

I'd write to Eily but I'm not sure of the address.

Yes K as you remark we <u>have</u> seen some good times but not as good as we might have seen.[21]

The UCD diarist described what it was like for those outside prison during Kevin Barry's last days.

Kevin was to be hanged on Monday and we all went up to Mountjoy where Father Albert said the Rosary, it was dreadful kneeling before the grim gaunt walls and knowing the tragedy which would take place next day. An armoured car patrolled the place, Canon Waters passed out looking disconsolate while Father Albert gave Kevin's last message to the University Students and to the 2nd medicals in particular. It was an exhortation to fight for the cause for which he was dying. And yet all that day we hoped for a reprieve – we spent our day awaiting the shout of stop-press, we made a holy hour in the Hall, our minds were given over to the stupendous tragedy. Next morning the Cumann na mBan went to Mountjoy to show their last respects to Kevin – I shall never forget my feelings when the poster 'He Must Die' met my gaze – then the grim tragedy really descended on us and there was not an unmoved countenance outside Mountjoy. That day a grey pall seemed to hang over the city – nature itself seemed to be protesting against the fiendish act, there was no gleam of hope – all was gloomy – deep, dark and miserable – everyone wore an expression of helpless misery and defiant sadness. Had we not prayed that day as we never prayed before I don't know what might have happened us. It was the first warning of the strength of the enemy we were fighting. We lost all our humanitarian feelings and actually rejoiced when later we heard three English officers would be shot for every Irishman hanged.[22]

General Macready resisted every attempt to have the prisoner reprieved. In his autobiography, *Annals of An Active Life*, he pointed out that the victims of the crime were also mere youths, one being younger than Barry, and they too 'left mothers to mourn their loss'. He could see no grounds for a reprieve. One British official commented, 'I can't see any reason to let him off if we are going to execute anybody – he was one of the party who attacked the bread lorry in Upper Church Street when they killed three soldiers, and Barry was identified as the man who shot the first soldier dead. He was caught hiding under the lorry, pistol in hand.'[23]

The final attempt to force a reprieve came in a letter from the Under-Secretary, James MacMahon, to the Viceroy, Lord French.

Your Excellency,

For the past 24 hours I have been importuned from all sides of politics in the country to bespeak Your Excellency's favour for reprieve of the convict Barry.

Though no one of the people who have expressed themselves as anxious for his reprieve finds any excuse for his crime, all write in the belief that his execution, however just it may be, will produce affects in the country as disastrous as those which followed the equally just executions that followed the Rebellion of 1916.

MacMahon 31/10/20

The next day the Viceroy replied.

> *My dear MacMahon,*
>
> *I duly received your note yesterday. I regret I do not share your views and felt myself compelled to refuse to exercise the prerogative.*
>
> *Yours very sincerely,*
>
> *French*[24]

On 28 October, nuns from the Sisters of Charity in Gardiner Street asked for permission to visit Barry during his last days. The nuns subsequently visited the other nine executed in Mountjoy. In the aftermath of the executions one of the Sisters wrote of their visits. The following is the account of their visits to Kevin Barry.

> Visits to Kevin Barry, RIP Aged 18.
> Executed Nov. 1st 1920.
>
> The first evening the Sisters visited him they said, 'Are we welcome Kevin?' In reply his face became radiant. He was much comforted by hearing them talk of God's love and intense interest in each one, and the wonderful meeting with Him so near at hand. These were the thoughts that filled the boy's mind. 'When a chap is young,' he said, 'it is hard to die, and it takes more than love of country to keep one up.' Referring to his General Confession he said 'I have a clean slate now, and I am glad to offer my life in atonement for my sins.'
> He talked but little, and after his death sentence came he would read none but pious books.
> On being told that we set aside one day each month to prepare for death, the grace we got struck him and he said, 'You must be very good.'

He was grateful to God for giving him such a chance of saving his soul. 'I have seen a great deal of the shady side of life since I came to Dublin, and I fully realise how merciful God has been in saving me from all this danger.'

In reference to some words which were quoted in the paper as having been spoken by him and his mother, he denied them. 'I would not know how to make up those speeches about Sir Roger Casement,' he said. When we were leaving that evening before his death he said, in cheery voice, 'Remember me to all who ask for me.'

He gave his mother a soldierly salute when she bade him a last sad farewell. He walked to his death unflinchingly.

May the prayers and tears shed for him bring the light of Heaven to his Soul.[25]

In the days before Barry's execution rumours of a rescue attempt were rife. Michael Collins had investigated blowing a hole in the wall of the prison through which the prisoner was to escape. On another occasion groups congregated outside to storm the front gate. However a rescue was not thought feasible.[26] One of the reasons for this was that additional security was supplied for the prison in the form of Auxiliaries under the command of Brigadier-General Crozier.

Crozier was the head of the Auxiliaries in Ireland. He had served in the Boer War and had led troops in World War One. Crozier became a controversial figure during his time in Ireland. After a number of his 'Cadets' (as the Auxiliaries were called in official circles) sacked the town of Trim, Co. Meath in February 1921, Crozier suspended them from their duties pending an inquiry. While Crozier condemned those under his command who took part in such actions his suspension of the Cadets was overturned by Major-General Tudor, the Chief of Police in Ireland. Crozier resigned in protest, the men were acquitted and reinstated with full back pay. One of the newspapers of the day commented cynically that the Auxiliaries could now go back to 'restoring civilisation'.[27] In his autobiography, *The Men I Killed*, Crozier wrote of Barry in very favourable terms.

I do not suppose that Kevin Barry, who was hanged at dawn one winter's morn in Dublin, in 1920, for shooting a young British soldier in a Dublin street as he guarded a military lorry drawn up by the side of the pavement, cared very much if his end were to come from the bullets of the firing squad or the hangman's rope. He was fighting for a 'right' against a 'wrong', against the cruel injustices of a system imposed on him and his in the sacred name of law and order and decent fellowship. Red tape demanded that as Barry had committed 'murder' in the eyes of the English law in that portion of Ireland over which martial law did not reign, he must be hanged. Had this boy, he was a university student, done what he did, in Munster, where martial law reigned, he would have been shot by order of a court martial. But under the Fascistic Act for the Restoration of Law and Order in Ireland, the commander ordered him to be strung up. In a properly constituted and Government-accredited war, where the 'rules of play' are different, he would have been a sniper. Had he, a licensed killer, been captured by the enemy, he would not necessarily have been executed. The rules of play for warfare would have ordained that he be concentrated safely in an internment camp until the end of hostilities.

I had a great deal to do with the last hours of young Barry's life, as it was my duty to supply a party of auxiliary policemen (ex-officers all), under a Regular Army officer of the Reserve of Officers, to watch over the lad in the prison cell so that the condemned prisoner might not commit suicide and thus cheat the hangman of his fee.

I visited Barry only once. When I did so I was reminded of the last hours of young Johnny Crockett [a British soldier executed for desertion during World War One] ...Crockett did what he did, in desperation, perhaps, to escape the cold and wet of a fire-trench during a grim winter campaign. Barry did what he did while fired by the desire to free his Ireland from what he considered an unfair yoke; with his eyes wide open to the facts and the consequences, he was prepared to forfeit his life in combat or by execution.

Neither of these lads whined. Had I had the opportunity I might have given Barry the chance I gave Crockett – of getting drunk in his last few hours. But I had no such opportunity; and, in any case, I very much doubt if he would have accepted the offer if it had been placed before him, because he was a proud boy. He was proud of dying for an ideal, for the freedom of Ireland. He was not sorry to leave this earth; he was glad to die as he was dying. Crockett, on the other hand, never disguised his sorrow at having to leave us.

In France I had no difficulty in finding a firing-party to shoot Crockett. But in Ireland, as no hangman could be found to hang Barry, we had to bring one all the way from England, in disguise, and in great secrecy. He came three hundred miles across the sea, surreptitiously, to hang a soldier of Ireland. You see so much depends on one's point of view.[28]

On the inside cover of Kevin Barry's official file in the Public Record Office, London, the following note was written by hand.

One of the guards who was with K[evin] B[arry] during the last hours before his execution states that Barry's conversation was largely on sporting subjects such as football and hurling.

He had never been out of Ireland and had very strange ideas about Eng.[land] He appeared to think of it as all one vast industrial area with no country villages or open spaces of countryside.

He stated that he considered himself unlucky at being caught...

Toward the end he lost all hope of a reprieve and remarked somewhat cynically that these were only known in the Cinema world. He went to the drop with callous composure.[29]

Freeman's Journal, 2 November 1920

THE HEROIC SACRIFICE

KEVIN BARRY YIELDS HIS LIFE FOR IRELAND WITHOUT FLINCHING

A BRAVE BOY'S FORTITUDE
HE GOES TO THE SCAFFOLD PRAYING FOR HIS FRIENDS AND ENEMIES

Kevin Barry is dead. He was hanged in Mountjoy Prison at 8 o'clock yesterday morning.

'A brave and beautiful death,' was the description given by Canon Waters, one of the prison chaplains, who ministered to the heroic youth as he was about to face eternity. He died with prayers on his lips for his friends and enemies.

Young Barry never wavered in the presence of the executioner and his assistant, and went to the sacrifice calmly and serenely.

Until the prison bell clanged out the grim announcement that the 'law had taken its course' there were many who had hoped against hope that reprieve would come, and to these the realisation of the tragic end came as a shock.

The mournful crowd outside the jail gate in the early morning broke the stillness only with prayer. And when Canon Waters appeared tearful and unnerved, to confirm the intimation given by the death-bell, the great crowd was deeply moved, and women wept and men were observed to control themselves with an effort. The request by the mother of the boy for the body of her son was refused, and he was buried behind the prison walls.

An inquest was forbidden by the Viceroy, and a military court of inquiry expressed the belief that death had been instantaneous.

Another young life has been given freely for Ireland.

'A Brave And Beautiful Death'

During the last hour of Kevin Barry's life the scene outside Mountjoy Prison was a moving one.

Many sympathisers with the condemned boy had assembled outside the gates at 7 o'clock and half an hour later about 2,000 people had assembled, none through idle curiosity, but all, with troubled hearts, come to pray for the passing soul. At a quarter to eight a company of Cumann na mBan marched four deep to the scene, and halted outside the outer gates of the jail.

In a lane at the side of Mountjoy Police Station a party of military was stationed. A double-turreted armoured car, with its guns turned on the crowd, loomed sinister in the mirk of early morning a few yards from the prison gates. Now and again it moved about the road, but always the gun-barrel protruding from the turret was trained on the crowd.

The Murmur of Prayer

As the fatal moments ebbed no sound was heard but the murmur of the people reciting the Rosary for the boy about to die. Old and young – men, women and children – joined in the prayer to the Queen of Heaven for the soul that was passing behind the grim, grey walls of the prison. Many made the responses in the Gaelic language, which the doomed youth loved so well.

And the armoured car menaced the people as they prayed.

About eight o'clock the prison bell began to toll its mournful message.

An Awed Silence

An awed silence fell upon the people. Women looked at each other with eyes full of unshed tears. The men bowed their heads still lower.

The death knell rang clear on the morning air. As it echoed over the heads of the people, the beautiful prayer of the Angelus was taken up by the people in brave steady tones.

The prayer ceased.

There was a tense moment.

The bell was still tolling.

In a little while it ceased.

A fitful burst of sunshine shone down as if to proclaim the passing of a heroic soul.

So soon was it born – it died.

The Clang of the Gate

The clang of the prison gate was heard, and a venerable, stately figure came slowly out from the grim building. It was Canon Waters, the prison chaplain.

With head bowed and tear-streaming face he passed among the people. It was a pathetic and dramatic moment. They pressed about him. 'Is he dead?' 'Did they hang him?' He brushed the tears from his eyes and answered simply, 'Yes.'

The agony of the women now found vent. The long pent-up tears overflowed all restraint, and on every side one heard the voice of passionate grief.

How Did He Die?

'How did he die?' they asked the grief-stricken priest. 'Bravely – I never saw one meet his death with such courage.' The gates of the prison avenue were opened and the people thronged to the jail gate.

The last scene of the tragedy was then enacted. A warder appeared at the gateway and affixed to the wicket door a brief typewritten notice:

'The sentence of the law passed on Kevin Barry, found guilty of murder, was carried into execution at 8 a.m. this morning. By Order.'

A cordon of police, under the supervision of an Inspector, now appeared, and the people were told to disperse. They refused to leave until they had said the Rosary for the repose of the soul of the poor boy.

After the execution the solicitor Sean O'hUaidhaigh sent the following letter to the Under-Secretary in Dublin Castle.

> *Sir, – I am instructed by Mrs. Barry, mother of Kevin Barry, to make application to you to hand over the remains of her son for burial.*
>
> *Please let me know where and at what time an undertaker on her behalf is to attend for that purpose. – Your obedient servant,*
>
> *Sean O'hUaidhaigh.[30]*

In the reply the Under-Secretary, James McMahon, stated that he was directed by the Lord Lieutenant to state that under section 6 of the 1864 Capital Punishment Act, it was regretted that the request could not be complied with. This section of the Act stated that the person executed must be buried within the grounds of the prison.

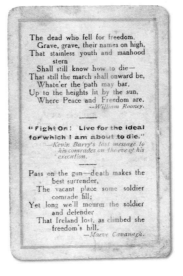

Kevin Barry's memorial card.

Deimhniú báis ar na h-eisiúint de bhun na hAchta um Chlárú Breitheanna agus Básanna 1863 go 1972.

DEATH CERTIFICATE issued in pursuance of Births and Deaths Registration Acts 1863 to 1972

Básanna a Cláraíodh i gContae _N City West_ i gCeantar an Chláraitheora Maoirseachta do _Dublin_ i gContae _City of Dublin_

Deaths Registered in the District of _N City West_ in the Superintendent Registrar's District of _Dublin_ in the County of _City of Dublin_

Uimh. No. (1)	Dáta agus Ionad Báis / Date and Place of Death (2)	Ainm agus Sloinne / Name and Surname (3)	Gnéas / Sex (4)	Staid / Condition (5)	Aois an Lá Breithe is Déanaí / Age last Birthday (6)	Céim, Gairm nó Slí Bheatha / Rank, Profession or Occupation (7)	Cuis Báis Dheimhnithe agus Fad Tinnis / Certified Cause of Death and Duration of Illness (8)	Sinniú, Cáilíocht agus Ionad Cónaithe an Fhaisnéiseora / Signature, Qualification and Residence of Informant (9)	An Dáta a Cláraíodh / When Registered (10)	Síniú an Chláraitheora / Signature of Registrar (11)
9	1920 November First Dublin	Kevin' Barry or Berry M. Mountjoy Prison	M.	single	18½ yrs	Medical Student	Execution by Hanging	Certificate received from military Court of Inquiry November 1st Nov. 1920 Inquiry held	1920	C.A. George first Cláraitheoir Registrar

Is fór cóip é seo de thaifid atá i gClár-leabhair Básanna in Oifig an Ard-Chláraitheora i mBaile Áth Cliath.

Certified to be a true Copy taken from the Certified Copies of Entries of Deaths in Oifig an Ard-Chláraitheora, Dublin.

Tugtha faoi Shéala Oifige an Ard-Chláraitheora an _seventh_ la seo de day of _June_ 2001

Given under the Seal of Offig an Ard-Chláraitheora this _seventh_ day of _June_

Ath-Scríofa Copied

Scrúdaithe Examined _MTM_

Is cóin trom é an teastas seo a athrú nó é úsáid tairéis a athraithe.

TO ALTER THIS DOCUMENT OR TO UTTER IT SO ALTERED IS A SERIOUS OFFENCE

Copy of Kevin Barry's death certificate.

KEVIN BARRY

In Mountjoy Jail one Monday morning
High upon the gallows tree
Kevin Barry gave his young life
For the cause of liberty
But a lad of eighteen summers
Yet no one can deny
As he walked to death that morning
He proudly held his head up high.

Why not shoot me like a soldier
Do not hang me like a dog
For I fought to free old Ireland
On that bright September morn
All round that little bakery
Where we fought them hand to hand
Why not shoot me like a soldier
For I fought to free Ireland.

Just before he faced the hangman
In his dreary prison cell
British soldiers tortured Barry
Just because he would not tell
The names of his brave companions
And other things they wished to know
'Turn informer or we'll kill you'
Kevin Barry answered, 'no.'

Calmly standing to attention
While he bade his last farewell
To his broken hearted mother
Whose grief no one can tell
For the cause he proudly cherished
This sad parting had to be
Then to death walked softly smiling
That old Ireland might be free.

Another martyr for old Ireland
Another murder for the crown
Whose brutal laws may kill the Irish
But can't keep their spirit down
Lads like Barry are no cowards
From the foe they will not fly
Lads like Barry will free Ireland
For her sake they'll live and die.

Kevin Barry you must leave us
On the scaffold you must die
Cried his broken-hearted mother
As she bade her son good-bye
Kevin turned to her in silence
And said, 'Mother do not weep
For its all for dear old Ireland
And its all for freedom's sake.'

Notes to the text

1. Donal O'Donovan, *Kevin Barry and His Times*, Glendale, 1989, p. 166.
2. Ibid. p. 11.
3. Ibid. p. 60.
4. Ibid. p. 57.
5. Courtesy of Donal O'Donovan.
6. Courtesy of Donal O'Donovan.
7. *Irish Times*, 25 September 1920.
8. Public Record Office (PRO), War Office (WO) 71/360.
9. For Terence MacSwiney's life and death by hunger strike see Francis J. Costello, *Enduring the Most, the Life and Death of Terence MacSwiney*, Brandon, Dingle, 1995.
10. PRO, WO 71/360.
11. *Irish Bulletin*, Vol. 3, No. 42, 28 October 1920.
12. General Prison Board (GPB) 1920, 9231.
13. Mountjoy Convict Reference File 1901 T.6.
14. PRO, Home Office (HO) 45/24753.
15. National Library of Ireland (NLI), MS 23,409.
16. House of Lords, Lloyd George Papers, F/180/5/14.
17. NLI, Leon O'Broin Papers, MS 31,658.
18. Ibid.
19. *Irish Bulletin,* Vol. 3, No. 4, 2 November 1920.
20. Costello, *Enduring the Most, the Life and Death of Terence MacSwiney*, p. 208.
21. Courtesy of Donal O'Donovan.
22. NLI, MS 23,409.
23. The Rt. Hon Sir Nevil, Gen. Macready, *Annals of an Active Life, Vol. II*, Hutchinson, London, 1924, p. 506.
24. NLI, MS 31,658.
25. NLI, MS Accession number 5140. Interviews with Mountjoy prisoners before their executions.
26. Frank O'Connor, *The Big Fellow, Michael Collins and the Irish Revolution*, Poolbeg, Dublin, 1979, pp. 121-122.
27. *Freeman's Journal*, 11 March 1921.
28. Brig-Gen. F.P. Crozier, *The Men I Killed*, Michael Joseph Ltd, London, 1937, pp. 124-126.
29. PRO, Colonial Office (CO) 904/42.
30. *Irish Independent*, 2 November 1921.

2

Thomas Whelan
&
Patrick Moran

'Bloody Sunday', 21 November 1920

On the morning of 21 November 1920, twelve British secret service agents and two Auxiliary policemen were killed by members of the IRA's Dublin Brigade and Michael Collins' intelligence unit, otherwise known as 'the Squad'. Most of the British agents were members of what was known as the 'Cairo Gang', because of their previous experience in the Middle East (they had been drafted in to Dublin to fill the gaps left by the assassination of many spies and informers by the IRA). The gang had been coming precariously close to damaging the republican movement; some of the key figures in the Irish Volunteers had recently escaped capture. On 21 November the agents were killed at precisely 9 a.m. (the two Auxiliaries were killed when they happened upon the scene of one of the attacks). Most were still in their night-clothes. Some were killed in front of their wives. Frank O'Connor in his biography of Michael Collins, *The Big Fellow*, paints a vivid picture:

> Sunday morning dawned bright and cold. A little while after eight o'clock groups of men began to converge upon hotels, blocks of flats, and boarding houses in the centre of Dublin. A discreet knock and they were admitted. Then a revolver was brandished in the servant's face, a guard was placed in the hall, and the men began to mount the stairs on tiptoe. Another discreet knock and a bedroom door opened and revealed a young man in pyjamas, his face still flushed with sleep. Seeing the tense faces and drawn revolvers, he threw up his hands and was pushed out of the room. In another room the men had forced their way in before the silence which had fallen since the bells of the city had ceased to call for nine-o'clock Mass; a young head fell back upon the pillow, and a red streak spread about it.[1]

Bloody Sunday, as the day came to be known, was a critical blow to the administration in Dublin Castle. Its spy and informer network, which had long been its eyes and ears, would never recover from the attacks of that winter morning. A siege mentality began to prevail in Dublin Castle with government officials increasingly reluctant to venture from the safe confines of the seven hundred year old citadel. But Bloody Sunday has also gone down in nationalist history because of British retaliation for the crippling of their secret service network.

A group of Auxiliaries.

That afternoon a group of Auxiliaries from Beggar's Bush barracks (the same barracks to which the dead Auxiliaries belonged) set off for Croke Park on Dublin's north side where a game of Gaelic football was being played between Tipperary and Dublin. Firing into the crowd the Auxiliaries shot seven people dead. Another seven were crushed to death in the panicked crowd. The British government long argued that the first shots had come from the crowd. Under the regulations of the time, deaths caused by the military were not the subject of public inquests but of military inquiries that were held in private. The results of the military inquiry into the shooting of civilians at Croke Park have recently been declassified. The contents of the inquiry reiterate the official line that the first shots were fired from inside the crowd. However, three important independent witnesses, all members of the Dublin Metropolitan Police who were stationed at the point where the Auxiliaries arrived, testified that the first shots were those fired into the air by the Auxiliaries. After that, general gunfire occurred. One of the Auxiliaries outlined his apparent involvement that day:

> On 21st November 1920 I was in the second lorry of the convoy to Croke Park. The lorry halted just over the Canal Bridge. I saw no civilians on the Bridge. There were some civilians in the passage leading to the turnstiles. I got out and went to the turnstiles as quickly as I could. As I got to the turnstiles I heard shots. I am certain they were revolver shots, a few shots fired quickly. They were fired inside the field. I tried to get through the turnstiles and found that they were locked. When getting over them a bullet hit the wall convenient to my head. This was the wall on the right hand side inside the archway and splinters of brick and mortar hit me in the face. It could not have been fired from outside the field. As I got inside I landed on my hands and feet. I saw young men aged between 20 and 25 running stooping among the crowd, away from me between the fence and the wall. I pursued and discharged my revolver in their direction. My duties were identification of certain persons. I was in plain clothes having a Glengarry cap in my pocket for identification by my own men if necessary. Having been fired at I used my own discretion in returning fire. I aimed at individual young men who were running away trying to conceal themselves in the crowd. I used a .450 revolver and service ammunition. I chased them across the ground nearly to the wall on the East side. I then saw that a number of people were going towards the main gate by which I came in. I rushed to that gate and took up my position outside to try to carry out my duties of identification. I stayed there until the ground was cleared, that is about an hour and a half.[2]

In the aftermath of Bloody Sunday, funerals took place in a number of districts. Nine of the British agents were transported to England for funeral services at Westminster Abbey and Westminster Cathedral on 26 November. Gun-carriages brought the coffins draped in Union Jacks in procession from Euston Station to

Westminster via Tottenham Court Road, Charing Cross Road, St. Martin's Place, Whitehall and Parliament Square. Each gun-carriage was preceded by a firing party, accompanied by pallbearers and followed by mourners. On arrival at the Abbey and the Cathedral one drummer and eight buglers of the Grenadier Guards sounded the 'Last Post'.[3]

As the funerals were taking place hundreds of Sinn Féin suspects were being rounded up by the police. The prisons of Dublin filled and Ballykinlar Internment Camp was opened in Co. Down. Eventually just two men were found guilty and executed. They were Thomas Whelan and Patrick Moran. Both strenuously protested their innocence.

In the following extract Mrs Whelan, mother of Thomas, outlines her son's brief life. This account was given to the nuns of the Sisters of Charity who visited Whelan in the run up to his execution.

> Thomas Whelan was born 5 Oct., 1898 in a cottage on the Sky Road in a small place called Gourtroma about 2 miles out from Clifden. He was one of a family of 13. Thomas was the 6th child of his Parents. He was loved by his 3 sisters and 9 brothers. In his early days he went to a small National School at Bayleek until the age of 12 years after which he graduated to the Clifden boys school until he reached the age of 15 years. He spent 3 years working with his brothers on his father's farm at Gourtroma. He spent many evenings fishing with his brothers in his father's boat. His whole delight was fishing and no matter his hard work he was always attentive to his religious duties.
>
> Thomas was loved by all his Neighbours and all who knew him for he had always a cheery word for everybody. At the age of 18 he went as a Messenger boy to Monsignor McAlpine P.P. of Clifden he removed there for one year after which he went to Dublin to seek a better living for himself. He boarded with a landlady named Mrs. Mann at 14 Barrow St., Ringsend. He worked at Boland's flour Mills, Ringsend

for 2 years. For the last 12 months he worked at the Broadstone N[orth].W[estern].R[ailway]. He was loved by everyone in Dublin that knew him and especially the People of Ringsend his whole leisure time he spent in practising singing to which he was greatly devoted and even in his lonely prison cell he was devoted to singing. The night before his execution he sang the *Shawl of Galway Gray* for the Nuns at 8 o'clock on Sunday night and he also sang at his own Mass at 5 o'clock on Monday morning just an hour before he mounted the scaffold. He was visited every day for the week before his execution by his Mother and many other friends. He was still happy and cheerful and told every one how happy he felt and of his innocence in the charge that was put against him but remarking, 'I hope God will forgive those who is responsible for the taking of my own life.'

He spent all Sunday night writing little souvenirs to all his friends and those were many and to his Father and Mother and Brothers and Sisters. Many of the friends who visited him in the Prison cut some of his hair as a souvenir and some of the clergy men who visited him cut some of his hair for a souvenir as he left a great impression on all the priests who attended him in Arbour Hill and Kilmainham and Mountjoy. He was arrested on 23 of Nov., 1920 and taken to Ballykinlar and remained there for four weeks. He was taken from there to Kilmainham and he spent 2 months there and was then taken to Mountjoy where he was awaiting his execution. He was executed in Mountjoy on Monday 14, March, 1921 with 5 other Martyrs.

RIP.[4]

Thomas Whelan was arrested two days after Bloody Sunday on 23 November 1920. On 1 January 1921 Michael Noyk, a Jewish republican solicitor who represented several of the men executed in Mountjoy and did much of Sinn Féin's legal work, was told to go to Kilmainham Gaol to take instructions for the defence of a number of IRA men including Whelan. Noyk met Whelan in his cell and thought him a 'fresh-looking country boy, full of health and vigour, with a fascinating and effusive manner'. During their first meeting Whelan informed Noyk that he had told a British intelligence officer that he was a member of A Company, 3rd Battalion, of the IRA. Noyk, aware of the desire to exact retribution for Bloody Sunday, was immediately apprehensive about the prospects for this defendant.[5]

On 1 February 1921, Whelan was one of four men charged with the murder of Captain Baggally at 119 Lower Baggot Street. In the attack Baggally was shot twice in the chest, once in the left arm, once on the top of his head and once in the back. An officer who occupied a room next to Baggally identified Whelan. He stated that Whelan kept him covered with a revolver while Baggally was killed. The other three men charged with Whelan were found not guilty of the charges brought against them. Their cases fell down on the evidence given by the witness who identified Whelan. Whelan was found guilty and was

Thomas Whelan, centre, and two Auxiliary guards, in Mountjoy.

sentenced to death. In the following article, the *Irish Bulletin*, an organ of the Irish Volunteers, outlined the serious flaws in the prosecution's case.

Volume 4. Number 34. *Irish Bulletin* Tuesday, 22 February 1921

THE CASE OF THOMAS WHELAN

On February 1st 1921, four men named James Boyce of 10, Aungier St., Dublin; M.J. Tobin of 19, Upper Sherrard St., Dublin; Thomas Whelan of 14, Barrow St., Dublin, and James McNamara of 81, Lower George's St., Dun Laoghaire (Kingstown), Co. Dublin, were charged before a FIELD General Courtmartial at the City Hall, Dublin, with the murder of Capt. G.T. Baggally, an English Secret Service Officer at 119, Baggot St., Dublin, on the morning of Sunday, November 21st 1920.

The prosecution relied for the conviction of [the] accused on the evidence of two witnesses: one an English Army Officer and the other a private soldier.

The first witness for the Crown was the officer who occupied the room next to that of Capt. Baggally. He stated he was shaving in the bathroom when he heard the armed men enter the house. He opened the door of the bathroom and was confronted by a man who ordered him to put up his hands. He subsequently identified that man as Whelan. Whelan covered him with a revolver and kept him in the bathroom for about ten minutes. Witness was able to see through the bathroom door and he saw a second man walking up and down on the landing outside. The other man he subsequently identified as Boyce.

The second witness stated he was carrying a message from Dublin Castle to Ranelagh on the morning in question. He was riding a motor cycle. He passed through Baggot Street about 9 o'clock and saw a group of men apparently leaving Capt. Baggally's house. He saw McNamara amongst the group. He recognised him 'by the back of his head and the way he ran.' He did not see his face. Witness passed the group and went on to Herbert Place. There he met the same or another group of men. They were carrying revolvers. They held him up. Among them was Tobin and McNamara. He saw McNamara's side face then.

Under cross-examination this witness stated that when he saw Tobin he was standing apart from the others. When he identified Tobin at the North Dublin Union Military Barracks he (Tobin) had a 'growth of beard'. Witness could not say whether Tobin was clean shaven when he saw him on the morning of November 21st.

He could not say whether the second group of men he met that morning were the same men he saw coming from Capt. Baggally's house. They might have been 'a different lot'. Witness admitted that the only feature he was sure of in the identification of McNamara was that he had red hair.

When the defence opened, Counsel for Tobin submitted that there was no evidence against his client. The Court agreed and Tobin was acquitted. Later a mass of evidence was produced – including that of a constable – to prove that McNamara was eight miles from the scene of the shooting on the morning in question. McNamara was acquitted. Evidence was given that Boyce was at home in bed on the other side of the City at the time of the shooting. Boyce was acquitted.

These acquittals are important in that the officer who identified Boyce whom the Court found to have been in bed when the shooting occurred also identified Whelan, and was the only witness produced against Whelan. The soldier who positively identified two men (McNamara and Tobin) as being present both of whom were found by the Courtmartial not to have been there, appeared at a subsequent trial [this was Patrick Moran's trial] and gave further evidence of identification which was accepted.

The defence of Thomas Whelan who vehemently protested that he was not at or near the scene of the shooting was then taken up. Five witnesses were produced to prove that Whelan was in fact more than two miles from the scene of the shootings at the hour at which they occurred.

The first witness who was Whelan's landlady, stated that Whelan came from his bedroom at 8.40. He left the house at 8.55 to go to 9 o'clock Mass at Ringsend Church. Baggot Street was thirty minutes distant from her house.

The second witness said she knew Whelan well. She saw him in Ringsend Church at 9 o'c. Mass. She was quite near him in the church. She saw him go to the Communion rails and receive Communion. She saw him leave the Church when Mass was over at about 9.40. Cross-examined she said Whelan had entered the Church before she did. She saw him in the Church when she came in. She could not make a mistake.

The third witness said he knew Whelan well. He saw him leave Ringsend Church at 9.40 a.m. on November 21st and go towards his home. He bade him good-morning. Whelan returned the salute.

The fourth witness said he saw Whelan come out of Ringsend Church after 9 o'c. Mass. Witness and accused conversed for some minutes. Accused then walked towards his home. The fifth witness was a Catholic Priest stationed at Ringsend Church. He gave evidence that accused received Communion at his Church every Sunday morning. He bore an irreproachable character. None of these witnesses was shaken in their evidence by cross-examination of prosecuting Counsel. Thomas Whelan was found guilty of murder and has been sentenced to be hanged.

STATEMENT BY THOMAS WHELAN AT HIS TRIAL

Gentlemen of the Courtmartial, all I have to say is that I am absolutely innocent of the charge that is brought against me. I can solemnly swear before God, I was never in 119 Baggot Street in my life, and that I wasn't in Baggot Street that Sunday.

For the past six or eight months I have been a weekly Communicant, and previous to that I was a monthly one, as I belonged to the Sodality in Ringsend.

I got up on the morning of the 21st November, and went to my religious duties as usual. That is I went to partake of what I believe and any other Catholic believes to be nothing less than the Body and Blood, Soul and Divinity of Jesus Christ. The Man who made me and you, what we are, and, who will be our Judge on the Last Day. Do you think for one moment I'd tell such a lie about the Blessed Sacrament, as, that in other words ask Our Divine Lord to shield me, as you term a murderer, or in plainer words to ask Our Divine Lord to commit a Mortal Sin, if that were true I would consider it by far a greater crime than the murder of which I am accused.

There is another point I would like to speak about. I now learn I was identified in Arbour Hill on December 1st two days afterwards I was sent to Ballykinler, and after an elapse of ten days I was served with an Internment Order saying I was arrested on Suspicion, and, that if I applied to the Advisory Court in London presided over by Mr Ross (Justice) I might, or I was liable to be released if they thought fit. Now do you think if I was what they termed me then a (Red Hot) murderer, only identified the previous day that they would send me to the Camp and give me this form? If I had got this form just when I landed I would imagine it had been issued by Head Quarters, and that it could not have been withdrawn, but no, I was there at least ten days when I got it, so that cant be no mistake. It just proves the strength of the Identification. (Turned to the Counsel) I also wish to thank my learned Counsel for the way in which they have defended my case. They done their best. They could do no more. [6]

At Kilmainham Gaol, Whelan wrote a poem and a number of letters to his sweetheart Pauline Swan.[7]

I

Oh the days were short and fleeting Pauline Dear
When as lovers we were meeting Pauline Dear
In dear old Dublin City mid people
Old and ditty and girls young and pretty Pauline Dear.

II

Our hopes were always cheerful Pauline Dear
They have ended now so fearful Pauline Dear
I know the news will grieve you
To say I'll have to leave you
Without being let to see you Pauline Dear.

III

Oh let not those tidings grieve you Pauline Dear
For though I have to leave you Pauline Dear
My spirit will be with you
That's all I can give you
They cannot keep it from you Pauline Dear.

IV

Though in a dismal Prison Pauline Dear
My hopes again have risen Pauline Dear
When I know it's all for Ireland
My own dear native Sireland
Sure I pledged my life for Ireland Pauline Dear.

[No date]   *Kilmainham Prison*
                                         Room 30

Dear Pauline,

Just a line hoping to find you in the Pink as I am at present thank God. I suppose you know by now the result of my trial. I was found guilty and sentence of death passed. Well Pauline I know you are sorry to hear it but its God's Holy Will and we must be satisfied. I don't mind it myself. I think of my mother most. She will feel it more than I will. As I'm innocent I have nothing to fear. I will die happy Please God. Now Pauline I wish to thank you for all your kindness to me most sincerely. I thought I would be able to repay you but we are now parted forever.

God watch over you and give you a long and happy life is my prayer to the last.

From Your old and Fond Friend Tommie

xxx

Love to mother and Lilly

From Tommy

[No date]   Kilmainham Prison
                                           Room 30

Dear Pauline,

Just a line hoping to find you in the best of spirits as I am at present. I know too well you are sorry for me, but Pauline there's nothing to worry over, I have a lot to be thankful for. I have plenty time to make peace with God and have the priests to come and see me. What more do I want. Then I have the many kind friends who call up with parcels including yourself to be thankful for.

Now Pauline don't worry over me dear, I will be happy soon if it is God's Will I'm to die as I'm innocent as you are. I will pray for you and your mother and Lilly in my prayers for the kindness you have shown to me. I was at Mass and Communion this morning, hope to go always while I'm here.

The Priest was surprised to see me in such good humour he said it was wonderful. When he asked me had I anything on my mind I said no. He then asked me was I ready to die I said, yes anytime. They wished to take me out now I was prepared. He gave me his blessing and shook hands with me twice, when I looked in his face I saw he had a look of compassion for me, and tears were almost in his eyes. Now I want you to do me a favour, as you know the photo I gave you, will you please get some copies taken of it and send them in to me I want to sign my name to them and send them to a few friends especially your mother and Lilly and of course yourself.

I feel now in the best of spirits you wouldn't think if you saw me, that I had been sentenced to death only a few days ago. I hope you are in good spirits also though a cruel law has parted us it cannot change my devotion. I will finish now with best love to all at home.

May God Bless and Protect you now and save you from all harm, is all I can wish you.

Good Bye From Your Affectionate Friend Tommie

xxx

[No date]   *Kilmainham Prison*

Dear Pauline,

Just a line hoping to find you in the best of health as I am at present thank God. I got your letter and Mr O'C too, I wrote to him again. Tell him I could read between the lines in his letter and that it wasn't meant for me alone to read, I leave it to him for that. I hope he is better by the next time [he] writes. Well Pauline, I suppose you have good times with his Mam she is my 'Foster Mother', do you know that's what I'll have to call her anyway for her kindness. I have your photo with my mother here. I was just wondering did the camera get broken I did not hear any account of it anyway. I had the priest in with me to-day… he said a mass for me yesterday. I don't know what can happen to me after all the prayers thats being said. You should see me with my bunch of violets in my coat yesterday and to-day. I must get a nice bunch for Sunday. It just shows you how I feel.

As I am in a hurry now I will close for the present. With kindest regards to all Lilly and your mother and of course all the old friends in No 14.

Good Bye now

From Your Fond Friend Tommie
xxxxxx

[No date]   *Kilmainham Prison*
                                         Room 30

Dear Pauline,

Ever so many thanks for the nice parcel received to-day. The dinner was just in time it was lovely. I gave part of it to two other boys, chums of mine, one is P. Conway, Mr. O'Connor knows him very well, the other is a nice little boy from Kilkenny. We share anything we get amongst one another. The[y] wish me to thank you when I'm writing. Well Pauline I got the games last Sunday and letters alright, also the cake and chocolates. I got everything correct to-day too, I didn't expect you to-day, as its really too good of you, coming down every Sunday. I was told you spoiled your dress to-day coming down, Thats too bad, I hope its not much. Well your photo with my mother is very nice you both come out good. The camera wasn't broken, was it? I got the photo's you sent in to-day all right there very good. I want to know Pauline was it you gave my photo to the press, as I thought they might have got it in my pocket Book and as I had one in it when I was arrested, my pocket Book is now in the camp I think. Let me know when you write again. I will finish love to mother and Lilly

From your fond Friend Tommie

In the review of security following a successful escape from Kilmainham by three prisoners Whelan was transferred to Mountjoy. On 5 March Whelan was informed that his death sentence had been confirmed. While in Mountjoy one of his guards, Captain Lester Collins, an Auxiliary, gave Whelan a box of chocolates. On Friday 11 March, Whelan was visited by his mother and Alicia Mann, an eight-year-old girl who lived in the Barrow Street house in which Whelan boarded. He informed his mother that his death sentence had been confirmed.

Whelan gave Alicia the box of chocolates and told her that if there was a late reprieve they could eat them together. If he was hanged she could eat them herself. The box was never opened and is now on display in Kilmainham Gaol Museum.

Mountjoy Prison   *10th March '21*

Dear Mrs O'Mara,

Just a line hoping to find you in the best of health as I am at present, thank God. I expect you know by now what my position is. Well, I am glad to tell you, that I never was happier in my life. Would you imagine that I still sing some of the old songs. I never thought I would myself, but it benefits me nothing to tell you a lie now. It is lovely to be ready to die, this world holds little pleasure for me now, I think of the next more, and indeed I won't forget any of you when I go there. I don't forget any of you even now. I pray for all alike, relations, clergy, friends and enemies. I hope everyone will get as happy a death as I will, that would be my wish to the end. My Mother is bearing her troubles bravely, but what are our sorrows when compared with the sorrows of the Holy Family. When my mother thinks of the sorrows of the Blessed Virgin, it will compose her a lot. I know too well you will be delighted to get this as P. Swan told me. I will send you some little thing as Souvenir. I am giving away little things all day long as Souvenirs.

Well Mrs, O'Mara, I never heard Mac Cormack after all. Do you know I would loved to have heard him. I always think of the songs he used to sing at 37. Well, I suppose Peggy is able to walk now, she will never remember me, but you can tell her she was in my arms often. Remember me also to Jack. I hope you will be successful in all your undertakings. Tell Gertie Webster I was asking for her also Mr Grey, and Kearns, Mrs Kane and Mrs Kinahan. I must write to her too. I would like to write to everyone if I could. The man who is bringing this to you I can never forget his kindness, he brings me chocolates and anything I care for, that's possible to get.

He will tell you how happy I am and how I took my trials. I was told today that Monday is the day of the execution, 14th March. Don't tell my Mother yet. She will know time enough. Goodbye now for ever.

Your Sincere friend.

Tommie XXX [8]

During his time in Mountjoy the twenty-two-year old Whelan wrote a melancholic poem reflecting his thoughts on what his mother must be experiencing.

God knows best! This is the cry of a heart
Broken with sorrow for her darling boy,
He dies for a crime in which he own'd no part;
A noble death in the prison Mountjoy.

'Tis His blessed will.' she mournfully cries,
As the tear drops roll down her care-worn cheeks,
'But 'tis for dear Ireland he bravely dies;
Proudly I give him tho' my heart it breaks.'

'Don't worry,' he cries to his mother dear,
As he bids her farewell in his prison cell,
'I'm innocent, so death I do not fear,
'Tis sweet to die for truth and country as well.'

With a cheery word and a smile for all,
A wonder to those who attend him there,
Forgetful of injuries both great and small,
For his enemies breathing a silent prayer.

The morn at last dawns dreary and cold
But his heart is filled with mystic love,
Soon the great God of Glory to behold,
To dwell in the mansions of bliss above.

Now all is over and his great happy lot,
He would not change for a kingdom of gold;
And as years roll by in each home and cot,
His name will be loved and his tale be told.

And steals o'er the soul of his mother dear,
A wonderful peace and an honest pride
For her boy whose name she will often hear,
Who nobly lived and splendidly died.[9]

At Mountjoy Whelan spent his last nights in a condemned cell with Patrick Moran who was also convicted of taking part in Bloody Sunday.

Patrick Moran was born in Crossna, Co. Roscommon in 1888. Although his birth certificate put his date of birth as 13 March he always celebrated it on 10 March. The third of eleven children born to Bartholemew and Brigid Moran, he went to primary school in Crossna and then served his time as a grocer's assistant in O'Rourke's, Main Street, Boyle. Moran went to Dublin in the autumn of 1910 and then spent a short spell in Athy; he returned to Dublin in July 1911. Until 1916 he worked in Doyle's pub at Doyle's Corner. Strongly involved in Gaelic football he was a member of the winners of the College Green Division of the Grocers' Assistants Gaelic Football Championship in 1913. On visits back to Crossna he would arrange matches between local boys.

Patrick Moran's Gaelic football team. Moran is first from left in the front row.

A labour activist Moran became involved in the 1913 Lockout (one younger brother was a labour activist and two were land activists). However, he was also committed to the nationalist cause. Moran was sworn into the secret oath-bound association, the Irish Republican Brotherhood, and was a member of the Irish Volunteers. In 1916 Moran was Adjutant, D Company, 2nd Battalion, of the Dublin section of the Irish Volunteers. During Easter Week he was part of the Jacob's factory garrison under Thomas MacDonagh. After the surrender Moran was sent to Knutsford Prison in England, then to Frongoch Internment Camp in North Wales. In July he was transferred to Wormwood Scrubs Prison and then released. He returned to his native Crossna in the first week of August 1916 but was soon back in Dublin.

Patrick Moran and and his sister B.

*Patrick Moran in
Volunteer uniform.*

oran worked first in Kingstown, now Dun Laoghaire, and was then employed in Magee's, Blackrock. In 1917 he became a founder member of the Irish National Union of Vintners, Grocers and Allied Trades, and was to serve as President of the Union and Chairman of its Kingstown branch. Moran also resumed his involvement with the Irish Volunteers. He became Captain of D Company of the IRA. Importantly, he was in charge of the port at Kingstown through which men, arms and information passed between Britain and Ireland. Moran was arrested on two occasions in early 1920 for intimidation and assault, first on James Brady, a publican in Kingstown, and then on James Smyth of Sydney Terrace, Blackrock. On 26 November he was arrested for a third time. On this occasion he was one of hundreds taken in on suspicion of taking part in the Bloody Sunday attacks. He was brought to Arbour Hill prison on Dublin's north side.

At Arbour Hill he was picked out by one Crown witness as being part of the group that had killed Lieutenant Aimes at 38 Mount Street, Dublin. A family memento that still exists is the collar of the shirt that Moran wore in Arbour Hill. After this identification Moran wrote inside the collar of the shirt, 'This place is the limit. I wouldn't be here at all but one young soldier thought he had identified me before which he hadn't. When he heard the name he said there's some mistake that's not the name, but the second soldier said 'twas me, so I'm here on suspicion. I wasn't in Mount Street for years so I hope the scales come off their eyes. Of course I can prove I was miles away but let them see their folly out, I'll make no statements.' After this identification in Arbour Hill Patrick Moran was transferred to Kilmainham Gaol.

No prison in Ireland is more steeped in the history of the struggle for Irish independence than Kilmainham. In August 1796, within months of opening, it received its first political prisoners. They were United Irishmen. In 1803 Robert Emmet spent his last night there before his execution on Thomas Street. Then came the Young Irelanders, the Fenians, Charles Stewart Parnell and the Land League campaigners. Most recently, the leaders of the 1916 Rising were shot in what had been the Stonebreaker's yard. When Moran was sent to Kilmainham he was put into what was known as the 'Murderers Gallery', where those suspected of taking part in the Bloody Sunday attacks were being held. This was in the old part of the prison; Moran's cell dated from 1796. It was just around the corner from the cells where Joseph Plunkett, Patrick Pearse, Tom Clarke and Moran's former commander in 1916, Thomas MacDonagh, had passed their last hours before their deaths in front of a British Army firing party. Today the story of Patrick Moran is a central part of the tour of Kilmainham Gaol.

Among those who were held in the 'Murderer's Gallery' were the five men who were fated to be executed with Moran on 14 March 1921. Also present was a man going under the name 'Stewart' but who was in fact Ernie O'Malley (later author of the classic war autobiographies *On Another Man's Wound* and *The Singing Flame*),

Frank Teeling, who had been convicted of taking part in Bloody Sunday, and Sean Kavanagh were also there. Ironically, Kavanagh later became the Governor of Mountjoy Prison serving almost continuously from 1927 to 1961, during which time he was custodian of the graves of his executed comrades.

During Moran's imprisonment he wrote a number of letters which have remained in family hands. What follows is a selection of the letters tracing Moran's thoughts prior to his trial and in the lead up to his death. This first letter is probably to Mary Farrell, the sister of his girlfriend B. Farrell. He described B. as 'one in a million'. B visited him regularly in prison, often bringing a flask of tea and apple-cake. In this letter he writes of his thoughts on being identified in Arbour Hill, and the belief that the suspicion on him would lift and he would be released.[10]

[No date]   *Kilmainham Gaol, Dublin*   *Monday*

Dear Mary,

I suppose you have heard of my change of residence and what a gloomy old pile this is. It would give you the blues. We had leave to shave in Arbour Hill but I used to use another chaps razor. We have to get our own one here. Will you call on Willie and get my Razor, Brush strap and Soap and a little mirror (to see myself as other see me) make all secure in a parcel and Post them on. I would feel down enough here if I weren't quite at ease about myself. I understand I am not here for trial but for a further identification test. I was questioned about a little street in Dublin Upr Mount St. that I haven't Stood in for at least two years and they didn't ask me for any statement which would prove it an impossibility for me [to] be there at the hour.

The Partial identification broke down but the Suspicion was enough to get me sent on here. Looks like being a very Happy Xmas though if they hurry matters up I might still be free then. I don't know for certain if they allow Parcels and Papers in to this lot of Prisoners. I would like some milk if you are sending anything and I must enquire about my washing. I don't want any yet though and might get Clare to call for it as she is nearer than you. I don't know of anything topical to fill up this space so must rush to a close. Remember me to B Peg and Pat also all my friends and you can assure them there's no need to worry about me.

With Sincerest best wishes.

Yours Sincerely,

Paddy Moran

Write soon we can get any amount of letters after they pass the Censor. I hope you will have Patience with me in all these distractions.

A t this point in the letter sequence the trial was postponed. Although Moran was not given the information, the reason for the delay was that an attempt had been made on the life of a Major Carew who was one of the witnesses who was going to testify against him. Carew had been sitting in a tea house on Dame Street when a number of men who were taking tea at a neighbouring table shot at him. Although he was hit, Carew was able to escape without serious injury. A witness to the shooting fired on the attackers who then fled the scene.[11]

Kilmainham Gaol, Dublin

Monday

My Dear Ciss and B [his sister Bridget],

I was very glad to get your letter and to know you are both so very well. I was sorry to see you were troubled as really though things may appear serious I know that such a charge can't stand the test of truth. I was thankful for the Prayer and Picture I had a lot of devotions before but am adding on those which I think Powerful. I had a letter from Mag they are all well. I never wrote to Miss McKenna and she wrote me.

As a matter of fact I stopped all my correspondents and am sorry now because letters are better than anything here. Anne has just been here with a parcel. I get too much food and often thought of suggesting that she shouldn't be going to the expense and then she has such a rush — while she could write as often as she liked. The conditions here have improved a good deal and everybody is feeling very well. I don't think I was ever much better myself. I should be sorry if anyone was worrying too much but as no action of mine was responsible for the charge being brought, I don't feel any personal responsibility.

The trial was to be next Saty [Saturday] but the Solicitor said that he couldn't proceed on that day so I don't know for certain when it comes off. In any case I am quite at ease on the matter. Write soon.

With very best love to you both.

Your fond Bro. Patk.

Once Major Carew had recovered sufficiently from his injuries, Moran's trial was rescheduled for 15 February 1921. However, in the run up to the trial plans were made for an escape from Kilmainham Gaol. The three initial escapees were Patrick Moran, Ernie O'Malley and Frank Teeling. While Moran was to be tried for Bloody Sunday, Frank Teeling had already been convicted. Ernie O'Malley was one of the most wanted men in Ireland at the time. There are a number of different versions of the Kilmainham escape, each of which contradicts the other in some crucial details. With the passing of over eighty years it is not possible to say which version of events is the most accurate. However,

Patrick Moran.

essentially the story breaks down into three parts. The first centres around the events preceding 13 February 1921 when, with the help of two British soldiers, Privates Roper and Holland, Oscar Traynor tried to get a rope-ladder thrown over the high walls of the prison (a group of four soldiers and three women who happened on one of these attempts was kidnapped and held in a nearby shed until the escape finally came off). When this attempt failed a second plan was hatched which involved smuggling a set of bolt cutters in to the prison to cut the lock on a side gate. The first attempt was on 13 February when Moran, O'Malley and Teeling actually made it to the side gate but the bolt cutters would not cut the lock. After modifications were made it was resolved to try again the next night. However, at this stage there was a crucial change in personnel. Patrick Moran's place was taken by Simon Donnelly who had only been in Kilmainham for a couple of nights.

Why did Donnelly replace Moran? As a captain of the IRA there was certainly no questioning the courage of Patrick Moran. In the published sources there is no definitive answer. Some emphasise that Moran believed that he would be found innocent. Others that Moran did not want to betray the large number of witnesses who were going to testify on his behalf. Perhaps a crucial change in circumstance was the arrival of Donnelly. Did Donnelly replace Moran for specific reasons? Whatever the circumstances the important point is that Moran stayed in Kilmainham Gaol, as Donnelly, O'Malley and Teeling walked out the side gate. To act as a diversion that evening Moran organised a sing song in the prison.[12]

The morning following the escape, in an atmosphere hardly conducive to good justice, Moran's trial began in the Council Chamber of City Hall, Dame Street, Dublin. Normally decked out with elegant furniture and imposing portraits the chamber was stripped down for the proceedings. Moran was tried along with Joseph Rochford for the murder of Lieutenant Aimes at Mount Street Dublin. Aimes was one of the leading members of the British intelligence network in Dublin. For the purposes of the court martial Moran was tried as a member of the Detachment 1st Battalion, the Lancashire Fusiliers, Dublin Castle. The trail lasted for three days. Rochford was acquitted, Moran's case hinged on the question of his alibi. Was Patrick Moran in Blackrock when Aimes was killed at 9 a.m. on Sunday 21 November as he claimed? In the following document the head of the court summarises the points raised by the defence and prosecution. Clearly dismissing the evidence of the defence, it was with the content of these notes that Moran was condemned to death.

NOTES OF EVIDENCE IN PATRICK MORAN'S CASE

A. The Prosecution

1. The accused was identified as having been present at the scene of the murder of Lieutenant Aimes and as having taken part therein by three witnesses and one Officer and two soldiers.

(a) The Officer, Major Carew, lived at No. 28 Upper Mount Street on the other side of the road to No. 38 where the murder was committed. Soon after 9 a.m. on being called by his batman he looked out of the window and saw a civilian holding up a soldier with a revolver. The soldier and the civilian went in at the door of No. 38 and the civilian just before going in at the door pointed his revolver at the Officer. The Officer subsequently identified Moran as being the man he saw though he is not prepared to swear positively to him. An attempt to assassinate this witness was made and the trial had to be postponed till he was able to give evidence.

(b) Private Snelling a soldier in the R.A.S.C. was the chief witness for the prosecution. He was held up by a civilian with a revolver in Upper Mount Street a few minutes past 9 a.m. When he first saw the civilian he was about 30 yards away and pointed a revolver at him. The soldier put up his hands and went towards him to within a few inches of him. The civilian told him to knock at the door of No. 38 four times which the soldier did. As the door was opened the civilian said 'open the door boys'. It was then open only a foot or 18 inches and the soldier was pushed in by the civilian who was holding him up. Subsequently he saw the murder committed in the house. He was left in the house and told not to tell anyone. He independently picked out Moran as the man who held him up. He had excellent opportunities for observation and is quite positive as to the identity of Moran.

(c) Private Lawrence was Major Carew's batman and living at 28 upper Mount Street on the opposite side to where the murder took place. Between 8.45 and 9 a.m. he looked out of the window and saw a civilian whom he subsequently identified as Moran walking up and down outside No. 38. Saw him sharpen his step take out his revolver and point it at an A.S.C. soldier. The batman ran and called his officer (Major Carew). The Officer and batman went back to the window. He saw the soldier standing at the top of the stairs with a civilian looking towards him. The batman went to fetch his revolver and subsequently saw men running out of the house. At a later occasion he picked out Moran from a number of men and identified him as the man walking in the street. He is positive as to Moran's identity.

B. THE DEFENCE

1. The following 8 witnesses:
   Miss O'Flannigan
   Mr McCabe
   Joseph Cannon
   Miss Aylward
   John Finn
   Mr Costello
   William Duffey
   Mrs Finn
   gave evidence that accused was at Blackrock 8 o'clock mass which was over at about 8.30.

2. Michael O'Connor and Mary Traecy gave evidence that accused was waiting for the tram at Blackrock about 9.30.

3. James Swan the Tram conductor gave evidence that accused got on the 9.30 tram at Blackrock and got off at the Pillar about 10 o'clock.
   John Mirrelon confirms having seen the accused on the 9.30 tram.

4. Patrick Hughes gave evidence that the accused was at a meeting of Irish National Union of Grocers' Assistants at 11 o'clock.

5. The murder was committed at about 9 o'clock. The evidence of none of the witnesses above referred to even if it were true would be really inconsistent with the accused having been at the scene of the murder which was about 2 1/2 miles away from Blackrock. The period from 8.30 to 9.30 is not accounted for. If the accused had a motor cycle, a bicycle or a horse conveyance and had been desirous of preparing an alibi for himself as Irish criminals frequently do he could have been at mass at 8 at the murder at 9 and back at the tram at 9.30.

6. There is only one witness whose evidence is really inconsistent with the evidence of the prosecution and that is Miss McGough the housekeeper at Magee's store where the accused lived. She says she gave the accused breakfast at 5 minutes to 9 and that he was at Magee's till about 9.30. Miss McGough said that 3 men breakfasted with the accused.
   Doyle.
   McCourt.
   O'Connor.

These were the essential witnesses to corroborate the alibi at the crucial moment. Two of these Doyle and McCourt were in Court ready to give evidence to support Miss McGough, but although the prosecution pressed the Defence to call these witnesses they were not called. The reason for this was that they had made statements to the police supporting an alibi wholly different from those which were put forward to the Court and the Defence became aware that the prosecution had their statements. [The court never elaborated on this point.]

7. The above paragraphs are based upon the assumption that the evidence of all the witnesses for the defence except Miss McGough could be accepted, but the whole of the alibi evidence was greatly discredited by the failure to call Doyle and McCourt and the mode in which it was got together. As to the mode in which the witnesses for the alibi were obtained reference may be made in particular to the solider who was asked in a public house when he had had a little too much to drink whether he knew Moran and saw him in Mass on Sunday 21st November. Reference may also be made to the evidence of Mr McCabe to whom Miss O'Flanagan directly suggested that he had seen Moran and herself on this particular Sunday in question.

8. Another defect in the alibi is that the evidence was to the effect that the accused got off the tram at the Pillar about 10 o'clock, yet he only reached the Hall where he attended the Meeting of his Society at 10.45. The interval is altogether unaccounted for.

C. EVIDENCE IN POSSESSION OF POLICE BUT NOT PROVED AT TRIAL

1. The police have a photograph of the accused in uniform of the I.R.A. with a pistol in his hand. This was found in Moran's room, but the man who found it was unfortunately not available as a witness at the trial.

2. The police have also statements from Doyle and McCourt who came to give evidence for the defence, but were not called, in which they prove an entirely different alibi from that set up at the trial.[13]

At the end of the trial Moran's defence counsel made an impassioned plea on his behalf. Addressing the six officers, who sat with their pistols on the table in front of them, he stated that 'there is one thing of more importance than the shortening of a period of temporary insurrection. It is that the eternal principles of truth and justice shall not be violated by those in authority; once they are so violated the result is disastrous to the entire civilian community.' He urged the officers to show real courage and put their hands on their hearts and say, 'No matter what I may think about this man's political feelings, no matter what I think I may have heard upon the evidence, upon the evidence I have sworn to consider the case. On the evidence I say he is not guilty of the charges brought against him.' [14]

The *Irish Bulletin* issued its own version of the trial which put special emphasis on the number of witnesses that Moran had putting him in Blackrock at the time of the killing. It claimed that Moran and Thomas Whelan had been condemned to death for no other reason than to allow Sir Hamar Greenwood, the Chief Secretary, to make good in the English House of Commons the boast that he had 'murder by the throat'.

Volume 4. Number 34. *Irish Bulletin*   Tuesday, 22 February 1921

THE CASE OF PATRICK MORAN

On February 15th two men named Patrick Moran of Main Street, Blackrock, Co. Dublin and Joseph Rochford of 11 Elm Park Avenue, Ranelagh, Dublin, were charged before a Field General Courtmartial at the City Hall, Dublin, with the murder of Lieut. A. Aimes at 38, Mount St., at 9 o'clock on the morning of November 21st 1920.

The prosecution relied for the conviction of the accused on the evidence of an English officer, his servant and the soldier who, in the last case, had identified two men as being present when the court found them to be innocent.

The first witness for the Crown, the officer, said he lived in a house almost opposite to that occupied by Lieut. Aimes. He was lying awake in bed on the morning in question when his servant rushed into his room and said there was trouble in the street. He got up and went to the window. It was then 9 o'clock or a few minutes after it. He heard firing. He saw a group of men leaving Lieut. Aimes house, he saw Moran among them.

Cross-examined this witness stated he could not swear that the man he saw was Moran. He admitted that at the identification his servant and himself were together and discussed the men paraded before them. He heard one of the soldiers present say 'Moran is the man.'

The second witness, a soldier, said he was held up in Mount Street at 9.20 by armed men who immediately afterwards entered Lieut. Aimes house. He recognised Moran as being one of these men. In cross-examination witness admitted that he had previously identified two men as being concerned in the shooting of Capt. Baggally both of whom were acquitted. He admitted discussing with an officer the men paraded for identification.

The third witness was the officer's servant. He said that he saw a soldier held up by a man whom he subsequently identified as Moran in Mount Street between 8.45 and 9 o'clock on the morning in question. He told his master he identified Rochford as one of the men he saw coming from Lieut. Aimes house after he had heard firing. He (witness) was accompanied by the last witness when he went to identify prisoners.

Cross-examined he said he knew the time because he heard the clock on St. Stephen's Protestant Church in Mount Street chime the quarter. (The Rector of Church subsequently gave evidence that the clock had not chimed for years). He said he had to wake his master to tell him what he had seen in the street. He was surprised that his master had sworn he was awake. The whole incident in the street lasted only from three

minutes to five minutes. The men had come and gone in that time. Witness saw Moran in the street from the top window of a four story house.

Evidence was then given which proved that Joseph Rochford was in bed, two miles away, at the time of the shooting. The Court found Rochford not guilty.

The evidence of the Crown against Moran then resolved itself into: – (a) the statements of an officer who had just risen from sleep, had seen a man for the first time on the other side of the street, and could not even swear that the man was Moran; (b) the statements of a soldier whose previous evidence of identification was found to be false; and (c) the statements of a second soldier who identified Rochford and Moran as being present at the scene of the shooting, and whose identification the Crown found to be false in the case of Rochford.

The defence of Patrick Moran was then taken up. Moran made a statement that he attended 8 o'clock Mass at Blackrock Church. He returned home before 9 o'clock. He was at his breakfast at Blackrock, Co. Dublin at the time of the shootings in the city. He travelled into the City on a tram car which he boarded at 9.30. He was first made aware of the shootings by the fact that troops held up the tram on which he was travelling. At 11 o'clock he attended an important Trades' Union Meeting over which he presided. The meeting ended at 1 o'clock and he went home.

Seventeen witnesses came forward to support accused's statement.

The first witness was a lady who said she saw Moran going into Blackrock Church at 8 a.m. She sat beside him in the Church.

She came with him from the Church and they walked together part of the way home. An English magistrate met her while she was with Moran. He saluted her. Moran returned the salute.

The second witness was a public man who said he had done more to beat Sinn Fein than all the English Soldiers in Ireland. He was a member of the Redmondite Party. He gave evidence that he met Moran walking from 8 o'clock Mass at Blackrock Church that morning.

The third witness was an English Government Official who said he saw Moran (whom he had known for two and a half years) at Blackrock at 9.30 on the morning in question. He was waiting for a tram citywards.

The fourth witness who knew Moran by sight but had never spoken to him said he saw the accused with a young lady entering the Church at Blackrock at 8 o'clock. He saw both returning from the Church after 8 o'clock Mass.

The fifth, sixth, seventh and eight witnesses gave corroborative evidence. Two were ex-members of the British Army.

The ninth witness was the Rector of St. Stephen's Church, Mount Street, who said the clock on the church had not chimed for years.

The tenth witness, an ex-soldier, gave corroborative evidence.

The eleventh witness was the housekeeper of Moran's residence who said she gave accused his breakfast at 8.55 and he left the house about twenty minutes later.

The twelfth witness, an ex-soldier, saw Moran going to 8 o'clock mass at Blackrock.

The thirteenth witness, a lady, said she saw Moran and a girl coming from 8 o'clock Mass.

The fourteenth witness, a tramconducter, said he knew Moran who boarded the first tram to the City that morning (9.30 a.m). He collected Moran's fare and stated to the Court the seat Moran occupied in his tram. Accused did not leave his tram until it reached its termination at Nelson Pillar at exactly 9.56 a.m.

The fifteenth witness knew Moran whom he saw on the top of the first Cityward tram on Sunday November 21st.

The sixteenth witness, a police constable, stated that no motor car came from the City to Blackrock between 6 a.m. and 9. a.m.

The seventeenth witness stated that Moran was Chairman of the National Union of Grocers' Assistants and that he had presided over a Meeting of the Union on November 21st. The meeting began at 11 o'clock.

None of these witnesses were shaken in their evidence by severe and lengthy cross-examination.

The Court found Patrick Moran guilty of Murder and he has been sentenced to death by hanging.

After his trial Moran was transferred to Mountjoy Prison. Until the days before his execution he was held on the ground floor of C Wing (the prison is divided into four wings radiating from a central 'circle', C wing is the third from the left). In this letter to Annie Moran, one of Patrick's sisters who worked in the Mater Hospital across the road from Mountjoy, Patrick expresses his shock at being found guilty.

*An aerial view of Mountjoy Prison. The hanghouse is the
small building at the end of the wing nearest the camera.*

Mountjoy, Saturday

My dear Annie,

I am writing this as my first letters since I saw you at the Castle. I came here last night and wasn't sorry to part company with that place. I think I had a rather unfair trial but the... was well loaded against me and I have a grudge against those who defended me in a couple of things that though they got me to write out the identification scene in Arbour Hill they did not at all cross examine the cyclist on the vital points nor didn't call a witness who could prove the scene. I am wondering now if this is really to be the last shift. It might and it might not. I need not have been there to stand my trial. If I didn't think I would be alright and I believe after all the prayers that prompting was for the best. I'd like to know how you are feeling about the present stage now and how all at home look at it. I never gave it a thought till I saw how worried people looked as I came out of court. I expect to get this out today, send a copy home and one to Ciss. We are allowed one official letter each day and I suppose there may be no limit to the number we get in. We can also get parcels etc but I don't want you to send in much. I want some hard plug and matches and some butterscotch. I suppose if there is any worry on either side you all are fretting for me and I am thinking of those outside and am A1 myself, so don't worry. Give my love to all round particularly B and Clare and all at S.C.R. I send all my love home and to Ciss and B. Remember the blackest cloud has a silver lining and I am not a bit downhearted. Get a permit at the Castle and come and visit me. I think it can be done. I gave your name, B and Clare first, also Peg Alward and Miss Flanagan. But there are so many I'd like to see I hate to make exceptions. With very best love and hoping to see you when the clouds roll by,

Your fond brother,

Patrick Moran.

[No date]   *Mountjoy*

My dear Parents,

I suppose indeed I'm sure you have all been anxiously looking forward to my trial and I know you are disappointed at the result. I was always so certain I would be set free that I was taken back myself. In fact I never thought the case would come off on the nature of the evidence I had heard against me, but my witnesses, though I had a host, seemed to carry no weight and it went against me. I've got so accustomed to consoling myself lately that misfortune and myself seem fast friends and we get along very well together. So for myself, I've no worries and I hope you will all rise to the occasion and don't grumble at the present outlook which might be worse.

I'm not guilty that's one consolation you have, and I expect things will right themselves yet. I saw Annie at the Castle when the trial was on. She is looking fine and is a brave soul though I'm sure she is worried now. I wrote to her yesterday and had parcels from herself and Clare [a cousin of Moran], at the rate stuff is coming in I won't have room in my cell shortly and there's no danger I'll be hungry, and I've kept my appetite all right. Now you must realise this is a hard sort of letter to write with so much uncertainty in the future, one can't settle down to discuss random topics.

You can keep hoping and praying for the Best and you won't be disappointed I'm sure. I hope you, B and Jim, Maggie and Joe are quite well and with best love to your dear selves,

Your fond Son,

Patrick.

Moran then writes to his sisters Cissy and Bridget.

[No date]   *Mountjoy*

My dear Ciss and B,

I've just finished writing a letter home and my word it was a hard task. I know they are sure to look on the worst side of the case and will undoubtedly feel cut up. I'm taking it for granted that you have heard the result of the trial which went against me. I was so full up of the idea of getting out of it that I hadn't given it much thought but I didn't get a fair chance from the other side and I thought my own counsel very slack.

However I have an easy mind on the matter and that's more than those who swore against me can. I know I needn't make any speeches to you to buoy you up in a difficult situation. You'll be satisfied to know I'm in the very best of health and spirits. I'm getting in too much grub from friends...and am feeling quite at home. I haven't stopped praying that right may be vindicated and I feel it will. Did you write to Miss Mc Kenna? Apologise for me and as I have plenty of time on my hands I may write her if she writes. Also Ccla Katie. Don't forget to write Soon, yourself and B. I have a few more here in the same boat as myself so am not too alone.

With very best love to you both,

your fond Bro,

Patrick.

Many efforts were made to secure a reprieve for Whelan and Moran. Joseph Devlin, nationalist MP for West Belfast, who provided one of the only voices of nationalist opposition in the Westminster parliament, raised the cases with Lloyd George. The vice-president of the 800-strong Union of Grocers' Assistants protested 'in the strongest manner against sentence of death passed on their President, Patrick Moran, in the face of overwhelming evidence for the defence, and we call on all lovers of justice to stop judicial murder'. The National Union of Railwaymen called for Whelan's reprieve.

Patrick Moran and Thomas Whelan with two Auxiliary guards.

These are the last three letters written by Patrick Moran. The first was written on his birthday. In it he asked his parents not to travel to see him.

Mountjoy Prison, March 10th 1921.

My dear Parents,

I suppose ere this letter reaches you you will have heard all the news there is to hear about me and I pray God to give you the grace to view my fight with death and my triumph over it with equanimity.

I was told today by way of a birthday gift I suppose that myself and another prisoner named Thos. Whelan are to go the same road as Kevin Barry went not long ago on next Monday morning. I know it will be very hard for you all to bear and I hope you will see it in the light that I do and bear it just as bravely as I do and as I will. Perhaps it is the will of God. I'm sure it is that I should get such notice of when where and how, my earthly course finishes and that I never again might get the same chance for a thorough preparation. I expect to die in the grace of God as I am now, I hope…and expect to meet you all in a brighter and better world and I want you all to look forward and to strive for that eternal reward. I had a visit from Annie…today. She will tell you how I feel about it, the question of whether anyone else should travel to see me was a sore one with me. No child ever had better parents, I did my best as a dutiful son and brother. I hope my efforts pleased God almighty and you. I feel strong in myself now for what I don't look on as an awful ordeal and a meeting with those I love so well might not do either of us good so unless you wish otherwise I shouldn't advise anyone to travel to see me.

I pray God almighty to bless you all. Don't worry for me, pray for me instead and shed no tears and always hold your heads high because I die a martyr not a criminal as they would paint me. Am rushing now, will write a few to Mag and the lads and yourselves, with Best love,

Your fond Son, Patk.

Mountjoy Prison, March 11th 1921

My dear sisters Cissie and B,

I meant to write each of you but I found the task hard just because I know what your feeling will be, not for my own, I'm feeling as well as you ever knew me.

After all the hopes, delays, connected with my charge I have to state at this period that on yesterday (my birthday) I was informed that a fellow prisoner named Thos Whelan and myself are to be executed on Monday morning 14th inst. You I know are quite satisfied with my innocence so are the public and I of course know I am. In this case I die a martyr and so does the other man. I am quite resigned to my fate and have trust in God's mercy and his divine will that this is perhaps his way of giving me what we all hope for and for what I have prayed for, a happy death. I pray that God may give you all the grace to bear this bravely, as you can rest assured I will.

I hope to meet you all whom I loved so well (and who were so worthy of a great love) in Heaven. I saw Annie and we agreed that it might be better for the composure of all of us that no one should travel to bid me good bye: May God Bless you all – shed no tears for me, pray for me and I hope to aid you all in your passage towards me by my prayers.

I can't express my love for you,

Your fond brother,

Patrick.

Mountjoy Prison, 11/3/21

My Dear Brothers and Sisters,

I write this on Friday night and I suppose you are not new to the news about my impending execution. I hope my loved parents and you all will bear the news bravely as you know I will and am. I should write to each one of you individually but those letters to loving parents, Brothers, Sisters, are the hardest of this trial. I am thoroughly [prepared] to die if it is God's will and might not again [get] a chance of making my eternal salvation secure. My (brother) prisoner Whelan and myself are very happy and give each other great help in our spiritual preparation. When we look on all the sudden and unprovided deaths which take place these times we might perhaps be thankful to escape such an end. It is arranged that it takes place at 6 am on Monday morning. Don't shed any tears for me but give me your prayers and I will aid you all in your fight to become united in the next world where a just and merciful judge will dispense justice and mercy.

I name you all in my mind and bid you a loving Good Bye.

To Moran and Family, Ned Doyle and Family, C Bruen and Family. I do the same and to all the neighbours and Friends, Mattimoes, Sheerins. etc, and Give them my love and remembrance. I should have to waste the whole countryside if I mentioned all the names I call to mind. Good Bye and God Bless you all. With my love and Prayers,

Your fond Brother,

Patrick Moran.

The day before his execution Whelan wrote a letter to his mother.

Mountjoy Prison

13th March

My dear Mother,

Just a line to let you know that I am still the same as you saw me today (Sunday). I was never afraid to die for a good cause. Do you think a mother like you would rear a son afraid to die? You are the bravest woman I ever saw. I am proud of you. There is many a man would like your spirit.

Of course I did nothing only what any man in my place would do — face death with a clear conscience and a good spirit.

It is a consolation to know everyone will have to die and face the One Judge, who will believe the truth and nothing else.

Then, mother, you and I shall be happy for ever. What is this world when we look at it as I do now?

I hope everyone gets a happy death as I am getting. You may be sure I am happy. The nuns were in to say the Rosary with us this evening, and I sang a few songs for them there. They'll find me in the morning game to the last. I hope all at home take it well too.

Good-bye now, mother.

From your loving son,

Tommie, for ever.[15]

Paddy Moran, Mountjoy Prison,
Mar 13th 21

Your fellow prisoners, like all the men and women of Ireland, are thinking of you always, and especially in their prayers. All recognize that the death to which you are doomed by the tyrant and oppressor of ~~your~~ our nation is an honour to you and we know that you are going to that death in the spirit of the best and bravest of your race.

The sacrifice you have made will pledge the men and women of Ireland to be faithful as you have been even unto death in the cause for which your lives are given.

Go neartaigh Dia sibhse agus sinne agus go dtuga Sé saoirseacht agus sonas d'Éirinn. Céad moladh agus glóire dá thoil ró-naofa.

[May God strengthen you and us and may He give freedom and happiness to Ireland. A hundred blessings and glory to His most holy will.]

Letter written to Patrick Moran by fellow Mountjoy prisoners Arthur Griffith, Eoín MacNeill, Michael Staines and Eamon Duggan.[16]

Memorial card in honour of Patrick Moran.

The following is an account by the nuns of the Sisters of Charity of their visits to Patrick Moran and Thomas Whelan in Mountjoy before their executions.

> When we went to the prison on Saturday March 12th, we were escorted to the condemned cell – the same in which we saw Kevin Barry, RIP, just four months before. Here we found Thomas Whelan. He was having tea and toast when we entered the cell. He beamed with delight when he saw us, and it was with difficulty we could induce him to finish his supper. 'I don't want to eat', he said 'When I have the Sisters and the Priests.'
>
> He told us that the bed at the other end of the cell was occupied by Paddy Moran, who was just then in the board-room with his friends.
>
> Tommy – as we called him, talked in a wonderful way of the glory that was in store for him. 'I just told my mother', he said, 'that as a

priest at the time of his Ordination starts a new life, so on Monday I shall start a new life which will never end.' He also said, 'The result of my death will be that my little brother Francis (aged 7) will become a priest: I wrote and told my Father so, and he replied that my wish would be carried out. My Father and Mother will never forget me, and when they are too old to look after themselves, they will have the consolation of Francis saying Mass for them.'

Soon his comrade Paddy entered the cell. He too was charmed to see us. Even before we arrived he had been quite reconciled to his fate by Tom Whelan's wonderful words full of faith.

Father McMahon told us that Moran's innocence was so clearly proved that he had not the smallest doubt of his acquittal. When the death sentence was read to him on Tuesday, he was very much shaken. Whelan said, 'Never mind Paddy, tomorrow you will be accustomed to it, and by Sunday you will not wish for a reprieve.' His words proved true.

Whelan also told us that what first reconciled him to his fate was, reading of the Death of the Little Flower. 'When I think of the weeks of suffering that little creature had to endure before her death, and here I am, going to Heaven with only a seconds pain if any at all.' (While we were talking one of the guards – a Black and Tan – was reading Tommy's copy of the Life of the Little Flower).

Both men calmly protested their innocence, yet freely forgave all who were concerned in their deaths.

On Sunday evening Whelan reported to me the words he had addressed to the court 'on that morning I had partaken of the Body and Blood of my Redeemer, and I would consider it a greater crime than murder, to do that if I were guilty and to bring the Lord Himself to shield me.'

When I spoke of the joy of his meeting with our Lord so soon, he said, 'I am thinking more about the Blessed Mother: sure I was lighting a candle to her honour at the fatal hour on Nov. 21st.' They derived great consolation from the likeness between their deaths and the death of our Lord. Innocent men sworn away by false witnesses and called to their Reward in Passion Week. They bore no ill-will towards any of those who wronged them. 'I am going before a judge who can make no mistakes,' Whelan said.[17]

Thomas Whelan, looking at the camera, in Mountjoy.

Notes to the text

1. Frank O'Connor, *The Big Fellow, Michael Collins and the Irish Revolution*, Poolbeg, Dublin, 1979, pp. 123-124.

2. Public Record Office (PRO), War Office (WO) 35/88.

3. House of Lords, Lloyd George Papers, F/180/5/17.

4. National Library of Ireland (NLI), MS Accession number 5140.

5. Michael Noyk, 'Thomas Whelan', *An tOglach*, Winter, 1967.

6. Courtesy of Whelan family.

7. The poem and all letters to Pauline Swan courtesy of Kilmainham Gaol and Museum.

8. Kilmainham Gaol and Museum.

9. Kilmainham Gaol and Museum.

10. All of Patrick Moran's letters are from the Moran family papers.

11. *Freeman's Journal*, 5 February 1921.

12. For some different versions of the escape see: Oscar Traynor, 'Three Men Walk Out From Kilmainham Gaol' in *Prison Escapes*, Noel Hartnett, ed., Dublin, 1945; Simon Donnelly, 'Escape from Kilmainham Gaol' in *Dublin's Fighting Story, 1913–1921*, Kerryman, Tralee, 1948, pp. 155-7; Ernie O'Malley, *On Another Man's Word*, Anvil Books, Dublin, 1979, pp. 259-281.

13. PRO, WO 71/363.

14. Ibid.

15. Kilmainham Gaol and Museum.

16. Kilmainham Gaol and Museum.

17. NLI, MS Accession number 5140.

3

*Frank Flood, Patrick Doyle,
Thomas Bryan & Bernard Ryan*

Attack on Auxiliaries at Drumcondra, 21 January 1921

After Bloody Sunday the War of Independence entered a new phase of intensity. On 28 November, less than a week after Bloody Sunday, a group of Irish Volunteers led by Tom Barry killed 16 Auxiliaries in an ambush at Kilmichael, Co. Cork. On 11 December, after a party of Auxiliaries had been ambushed on the outskirts of Cork, the city was looted and many of its buildings, including City Hall, were burned in reprisal by Black and Tans. This was the last of the large-scale unofficial reprisals. In their place were official reprisals against the property of well-known members of Sinn Féin.

Burning of Cork City.

Burning of Cork City.

In the new year one newspaper began a grim daily tally of the killed and wounded on both sides. In Dublin the IRA abandoned its policy of not staging an attack when civilians would be endangered, and the city became a major centre of operations. According to the author Piaras Beaslai, 'firing for hours after Curfew, with no apparent objective, was a common occurrence… The roar of bombs, and the report of guns were familiar sounds to the ears of all, by day and by night, and the most peaceful and unwilling citizen learned to distinguish between the sound of a revolver, a rifle, a machine gun and a bomb.'[1] According to one contemporary, 'shootings and ambushes were becoming the order of the day… Explosions, mysterious firing and counter-firing became nightly occurrences but soon they ceased to disturb our slumbers.' In Dublin in the first three weeks of January 1921, a police District Inspector was killed on O'Connell Street, military officers were fired on at Charlemont Bridge (their car was riddled with bullets), a number of IRA men were arrested after an arms find, bombs were thrown and shots fired at an Auxiliary patrol near Bachelor's Walk, a man was shot and wounded in the Empire Theatre, bombs were thrown at Auxiliary police at Merrion Square, shots were exchanged between Auxiliaries and armed men at Dundrum, bombs were thrown at Crown forces at Parliament Street, and shots were fired at them at Portobello and Summerhill.[2] On 22 January 1921, the following article appeared in the *Irish Independent*.

Irish Independent, 22 January 1921

AMBUSH FAILS IN DUBLIN
ATTACK ON LORRY OF R.I.C. MEN
A CIVILIAN WOUNDED
FIVE ARRESTS MADE IN DRUMCONDRA

Shortly after 11 a.m. yesterday, an attempt to ambush Crown forces, it is officially stated, was made unsuccessfully by some young men near the Tolka bridge, Drumcondra.

Varying accounts of the occurrence are given, but it is certain that one civilian, Francis Flood (20), was seriously wounded [the extent of Flood's injuries were exaggerated, he attempted to get word to his family to allay their fears], he and 4 other civilians being subsequently arrested. The Crown forces suffered no casualty.

No Crown Casualties

Story of the Fight at Tolka Bridge

The military communiqué issued from headquarters yesterday says: 'At 11:30 a.m. on the Drumcondra Road, in the vicinity of the bridge over the Tolka, a military lorry of the R.I.C. was ambushed. A party of Auxiliaries immediately arrived on the scene, and captured five ambushers, all of whom were in possession of arms and bombs. One of the ambushers was badly wounded. The Crown forces suffered no casualties.'

Some people in the vicinity of the Tolka bridge stated that two cars, with Crown forces, came down the hill rapidly from Whitehall direction, and before the first reached the bridge revolver fire was opened on them, while two attackers, going close to the cars, threw at them 2 bombs, which exploded with great noise and force.

Dash down Richmond Road

It is said that several of those on one of the lorries were seen to fall, their headgear being blown into the air. The leading car, however, kept on and crossed the bridge, and 3 or 4 men carrying revolvers disappeared from the main thoroughfare, dashing down Richmond Rd.

A lady wheeling a perambulator in Richmond Rd. at the time, apparently came in the zone of fire, but was not injured.

Shortly after the attack a large force of Auxiliaries, with an armoured car, arrived on the scene, and a thorough search of the plots in Clonturk Park, which was covered by guns of the car, was made, and it was alleged that two men were shot, one being a member of the Auxiliary force.

This statement regarding the Auxiliary, however, is not borne out in the official report.

Auxiliary Reinforcements

It is stated in another report that on Drumcondra Rd., on the city side of the bridge, they either turned back or informed another force outward bound, and these appeared at the scene of the attack and opened fire towards Clonturk Park. A man who, it was said, was working on a plot in the park at the rear of Shamrock Villas, Drumcondra Rd., was badly wounded in the legs.

He was taken by Auxiliaries into the yard of one of the houses, where he was supplied with a drink of water, and then brought through the house to the front, where he was placed on a Crossley lorry and removed to a destination which was not disclosed.

According to a spectator, the wounded man appeared to be in great pain, but was quite conscious. He seemed to be bleeding profusely before being placed in the lorry, the point at which the vehicle drew up being marked with large bloodspots.

In the subsequent search, in which the arrests were made, motor cars from and to the city were held up and searched, but the forces withdrew shortly after noon.

How Captures were made

A further report states that apparently Dublin Castle had been acquainted of the assembly of some young men at Tolka bridge. Forces were at once dispatched to the spot, these dividing and proceeding by different routes.

One contingent approached the bridge direct whilst the other went via Richmond Road and Grace Park Road, and, it is stated, that it was on the Grace Park Road side of Clonturk Park that the captures were effected.

It is also said that walls on the Grace Park Road side had been extensively loop-holed, and that at this spot were discovered a quantity of small bombs and revolver ammunition. Each of those captured, it was further alleged, carried two automatic revolvers.

A young lad, who was on the spot at the time, says that after the explosions he saw young men run across the Park towards Grace Park Road, and he then heard shots. Labourers working on Grace Park Road were held up by the forces on their arrival and searched.

The wounded man is Francis Flood, aged about 20, a University engineering student residing at Summerhill. His house was subsequently raided. The names of the others arrested were not made known up to last night.

On one side of the bridge is a mark which might have been caused by a bomb.

On 23 February, Frank Flood, Patrick Doyle, Thomas Bryan and Bernard Ryan were charged with the attack at Drumcondra.

Frank Flood was 19 years old at the time of his arrest. He lived at 30 Summerhill Parade where his family ran a shop. Educated at the Christian Brothers' School, North Richmond Street, he was remarked to be a gentle youth who was fond of his studies. He obtained two Exhibitions in the Intermediate Certificate, one in Junior and another in Middle Grade. He won a scholarship to college and at the time of his arrest was a second year engineering student at UCD (he had passed his first

Frank Flood.

and second year exams with distinction). In another year he would have obtained his degree. A friend of Kevin Barry, he was, like Barry, young, good-looking, bright and had what seemed a promising future ahead of him. Flood was from a strongly republican family with three of his brother's active members of the Dublin Brigade. His brother Tom was later captured in the Customs House attack in May 1921, and was sentenced to death. However, he was saved from execution by a bout of tuberculosis and by the calling of the Truce. Like Barry, while attending his studies Frank had also joined the Irish Volunteers. He rose to the rank of Lieutenant, H Company, of the Dublin Brigade, IRA. When measures were being taken against the British forces Frank had volunteered for active service. He took part in the King's Inn raid with Barry, as well as in the Church Street attack in which Barry was captured. Prior to his execution Barry wished Flood a long and prosperous life. He was part of the crowd outside Mountjoy during his friend's execution. Later when he himself was in a condemned cell in Mountjoy he reflected ironically on Barry's parting blessing. Flood asked to be buried as close as possible to Barry.

At the time of the attack Patrick Doyle was 29 years old. He lived at 1 Saint Mary's Place. Born in Portland Row he had attended North William Street primary school, and then O'Connell's school. A carpenter by trade he was a founding member of the Amalgamated Society of Carpenters, Cabinetmakers and Joiners. Doyle was a great singer, a favourite song of his was the *Rose of Tralee*. He was also a keen sportsman and had won the Leinster Junior Football League 1912–13 with Seaview. In 1916 he married his wife Louisa Herbert who was from Glasgow. In 1917 their first child was born. She was christened Catherine Constance (after Constance de Markievicz) but was called Kathleen. She was the apple of her father's eye. In 1919 a son, Patrick, was born but he died of pneumonia in October 1920. On 27 February 1921, Louisa gave birth to twin girls. Doyle was a member of F Company, 1st Battalion, of the Dublin Brigade. He had been active since at least March 1919 when he took part in a raid for arms at Collinstown Camp. He was originally ruled out from this potentially dangerous assignment

Patrick Doyle.

Thomas Bryan.

because he was married with children, but he dismissed such concerns and the attack was planned at his home in Saint Mary's Place. Like several of the others executed at Mountjoy, Doyle was not the only member of his family involved in the republican movement. His brother Sean was also a Volunteer who died after being wounded in the Custom's House attack of May 1921.

Thomas Bryan was 22 years old and lived at 14 Henrietta Street. He was educated at the Christian Brothers' school, North Brunswick Street. An electrician by trade he had married Annie Glynn only a month before his arrest; he had waited to marry her until he was in a suitable financial position. Although still young, Bryan had been in the Volunteers for a number of years and had taken part in the 1917 Mountjoy hunger strike in which Thomas Ashe died. Subsequently Bryan had come to the attention of the Crown forces a number of times. Once he was being interrogated by a British soldier who had just seen Bryan's mother at Henrietta Street. Bryan was in good form and was laughing and joking. The officer slapped him across the face with his gloves and reportedly said, 'Tommy, you little brat, your mother is worried up there, worried sick over you, and here you are laughing and joking.' Another time he was on his bicycle when he was chased by troops. He abandoned the bicycle and escaped over a wall. However, abandoning the bicycle was a potentially dangerous move. Bicycles were a favourite mode of transport for the IRA and when one was purchased the name and address of the buyer were noted in a ledger beside the number of the bicycle. To stop it being traced back to him Bryan contacted his comrades who broke into the shop and took the incriminating records. He was very close to his sister Bridget who was also a republican and a member of Cumann na mBan.

Bernard Ryan was 20 years old and was an apprentice tailor. He lived at 8 Royal Canal Terrace, Phibsboro, with his elderly and widowed mother. He was educated at Saint Gabriel's School, Cowper Street, and later received private tuition at home. He qualified as a government official but became a clerk in a city firm. From then on he was the breadwinner for his elderly mother and sister who was too delicate to work. A keen sportsman he played Gaelic football and had won a number of medals for swimming. He had a quiet personality and when he spoke he was always to the point. In November 1920, he was in Croke Park on Bloody Sunday. A student of the Irish language, his teacher later wrote, 'Little did we, who sat with him during

Bernard Ryan.

his last session in our Fainne Group, think that even as we talked of Kevin Barry's heroic death, one amongst us was soon to make the same sacrifice.'[3] Ryan was a member of 1st Battalion, F Company, Dublin Brigade.

Flood, Doyle, Bryan and Ryan were held in the 'Murderer's Gallery' in Kilmainham Gaol until they were moved to Mountjoy following the escape of 14 February. While in Kilmainham Thomas Bryan, on his fifteenth day of imprisonment after being informed of the evidence against him, penned the following poem in which he pondered his future and expressed the hope of being reunited with his young wife.

1

On a bed made of planks and a pillow of hair
I lie down to sleep but no rest I find there,
I am thinking of home and the joys of my life
And the sweet little Colleen I now call my wife,
Of ...., all, I am nearly bereft,
My life or my honour, oh which will be left.

2

I've got one consolation, I believe when I pray
To the King of all kings, that he'll win me the day,
I plead and I pray to my Mother on high
To ask God to save me, for I don't want to die,
But to live for my wife and the dear little child
Who is coming to guide us to God's blessed side.

3

My wife and my people, I know how they pray
To our Lord and his Mother, by night and by day,
To guard and protect me right through the fight
For Ireland and Freedom, and Justice and Right.
I know that He'll save me and spare me my life
To be happy once more with my dear little wife.[4]

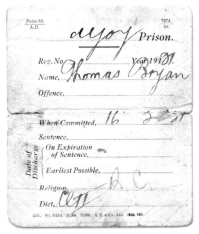

Thomas Bryan's Mountjoy commital card.

O n his second day in Mountjoy, Bernard Ryan wrote a letter to his mother.

Mountjoy 17 Feb. 1921

Dear Mother,

I suppose you are not surprised to see that I have changed my address. I just came here last night but I was left Kilmainham on Tuesday. I thought I would have been able to let you know before Wednesday and save you that terrible journey but I couldn't. However, this place is very convenient to you now.

I think they will take parcels any day here, but they must only contain foodstuffs so don't bring up any underclothing. When you are coming up don't bother about bread as I have plenty for the present. This is owing to the fact I didn't get time to eat it. Bring up some butter and salt and a bit of sweet cake.

I am in the best of health and I hope you are the same. Tell Sarah I was asking for her also Katie, Jack, Agnes and Paddy.

No more news at present and I am in a hurry to get this posted as soon as possible.

Your Loving Son

Berty.[5]

T he trial of the four men captured at Drumcondra differed in one fundamental way from the trials of the others executed at Mountjoy; no one died in the attack they were accused of taking part in. Although the men could not be tried for murder, the capture of IRA men, apparently on active service, was a rare occurrence which the Crown sought to exploit to the full. The men were charged with high treason. It carried the death sentence. They were the first Irish people to be tried for treason since Sir Roger Casement was tried in the Old Bailey in 1916. At their trial in City Hall the specific charges against the four were spelled out.

1. That accused, knowing the existence of a treasonable combination called the Irish Republican Army, or the Irish Volunteers, having for one of its objects the levying of war against the King, assembled, with other persons unknown, in, or near, Drumcondra Rd., armed with firearms and explosives with intent to use them in furtherance of the object aforesaid.

2. Conspiracy to levy war.

3. Assembly with intent to use fire arms.

4. Loop-holed a wall at, or near, Clonturk Park, for the purpose of ambushing and by force attacking the King's forces.

5. Attacking the forces with explosives and firearms.

6. Shooting at members of the Auxiliary Division of the RIC with intent to levy war against the King.[6]

The trial lasted two days. The defence called no witnesses. The defence counsel primarily attacked the weaknesses of the prosecution case. The main points made were that there was no evidence that the men had played a direct role in the attack and that there were no witnesses to connect them with those who had thrown the bombs. They were merely in an area in which an attack had taken place. The only evidence against them that they had 'levied war' were the shots which were fired when they were fleeing from the Auxiliaries. The defence stated that these three shots were fired in a desperate attempt by the men to save their lives; one of the shots was at a lock on a gate. However, the prosecution described these acts of retreat as 'waging war'. They contended that the actions of the handful of men running down Grace Park Gardens were just as much acts of war as the retreat of a great army on a field of battle in the Great War. For the prosecution the fact that they were caught running from the scene of the ambush, and that they were armed at that time, were strong arguments.

SUMMING UP

THE JUDGE ADVOCATE: Colonel Powell and gentlemen, you are now called upon to decide issues of a very grave and unusual nature.

As you have been informed, the crime of high treason is governed by one of the very oldest of our Criminal Statutes dating from the year 1351, and so far as Ireland is concerned, since the year 1494, when it was applied by Poyning's Act to Ireland. There are, as you are probably aware, various forms of high treason, but in this case you are concerned with only one of them, that of levying war against the King in his realm. Treason is an offence committed against the duty of allegiance, and a breach of that duty by a natural born subject of the Crown renders the offender liable to be proceeded against for high treason. It is the established law that if a man levies war against the King in the United Kingdom he can be convicted of and punished for high treason…

Gentlemen, I do not disguise from you the sense of responsibility I feel in submitting to you a statement of the law in so unusual and in many respects so difficult a matter as that of high treason. Learned Counsel for the Crown and for the Defence have more than once dealt with the law of high treason, and I think you have it clearly before you. I only propose to read one sentence in addition to what they have read, from a work which though 125 years old is yet 300 years or more more modern than the Statute under which the accused are tried. I suppose no-one will venture to question the authority of a work like Hawkins' Pleas for the Crown. This is the passage:

> *'It is to be observed that not only those who directly rebel against the King and take up arms in order to dethrone him, but also in many other cases those who in a violent and forcible manner withstand his lawful authority, or endeavour to reform his government, are said to levy war against him.'*

Let me say now a few words as to the objects which it is alleged by the Crown that the accused and those associated with them had in view in the operations which have been deposed to in evidence – that is to say if you are satisfied that it was the accused who were concerned. The Prosecution have sought to prove the existence in Ireland of a treasonable combination called the Irish Republican Army, or the Irish Volunteers, whose general aim it is to promote rebellion by force of arms, to establish a Republic in Ireland and separate her from the United Kingdom. They have sought to show that these accused persons were well aware of this treasonable conspiracy, and in conjunction and combination with others like minded to themselves, had contributed their own share to this treasonable conspiracy, and had on the 21st January assembled together at or in the neighbourhood of Drumcondra Road and Clonturk Park armed with firearms and explosives, had loopholed a wall for the purpose of ambushing the Forces of the Crown, and had actually attacked them there and subsequently in Grace Park Road. Gentlemen, if you are satisfied that the object of the accused (if you think it was the accused) was to bring about, in combination with others, by acts of violence, the overthrow of the existing regime in Ireland, you would be justified in law in coming to the conclusion that they were levying war against the King within his realm. Oral evidence has been given before you of the existence of the treasonable conspiracy to which I have referred. You have had called here in Court an official witness who speaks of his official knowledge of these matters, and who has produced to the Court certain documents tending to show that a state of rebellion existed on the date of the offence charged against the accused...[7]

After two days the military court found all four guilty of levying war against the King. Their case highlighted the conflicting views held by the two sides on certain fundamental issues. Although the prosecution went to great lengths to prove that the men had carried out acts of war, the men were sentenced to death and were ultimately hanged like criminals. The men were charged with treason by a court which represented to them an alien and unwelcome government.

The four were handed a form filled in by the President of the court informing them of their death sentence (a fifth, Dermot O'Sullivan, was also found guilty but his death sentence was commutted to penal servitude for life because he was just 17).

INSTRUCTIONS FOR THE GUIDANCE OF COURTS MARTIAL WHERE A SENTENCE OF DEATH HAS BEEN PASSED

To ....

The Court have found you guilty of the following charges____

High Treason..

....

~~but not guilty of the following~~____

....

The Court have passed a sentence of death upon you.

The Court have made no recommendation of mercy ~~in the following terms.~~

You should clearly understand:

(i) That the finding or findings and sentence are not valid until confirmed by the proper authority.

(ii) That the authority having power to confirm the finding or findings and sentence may withhold confirmation of the finding or findings, or may withhold confirmation of the sentence, or may mitigate, commute or remit the sentence, or may send the finding or findings and sentence back to the Court for revision.

If you do not clearly understand the foregoing you should request to see an officer, who will fully explain the matter to you.

PLW Powell Lt.Col. [signed]President

General   Court Martial

Dublin   Place

24/2/21   Date[8]

The day after the trial ended Thomas Bryan wrote to his father-in-law.

> Thomas Bryan
>
> Mountjoy Prison
> Dublin
> 25/2/21
>
> Dear Dick
>
> Just a few lines hoping you & all at home are in the pink. as this leaves me thank God. well Dick my trial is over & I have received my Death Sentence but it is not confirmed yet but that is only a matter of time. I have not told Annie my Sentence needless to say & I dont know how to do so. I pray that God may give Her Strength to bear this heavy Cross. I have asked Her to inquire about a visit as my trial is over She may be allowed one Personally. I dont mind Death in any form but naturally my thoughts stray to my Dear little Wife for as she truely said some time ago its our Women who suffer the most I dont intend to say anything to Annie re my Sentence untill I see if it is possible to get a visit. I would like to see Her by Herself for a while. afterwards I will let my Her people know. I wonder how She will take it God give them all strength to bear it. well Dick I know you will do your best to keep Her spirits up it is quite possible my Sentence

Thomas Bryan

Mountjoy Prison
Dublin
25/2/21

Dear Dick,

Just a few lines hoping you and all at home are in the pink as this leaves me thank God. Well Dick my trial is over and I have received my Death Sentence but it is not confirmed yet but that is only a matter of time. I have not told Annie my Sentence needless to say and I dont know how to do so. I pray that God may give Her Strength to bear this heavy Cross. I have asked her to inquire about a visit as my trial is over She may be allowed one Personally. I dont mind Death in any form but naturally my thoughts stray to my Dear little Wife for as she truely said some time ago its our Women who suffer the most. I dont intend to say anything to Annie re my Sentence until I see if it is possible to get a visit. I wonder how she will take it. God give them all strength to bear it. Well Dick I know you will do your best to keep her spirits up. It is quite possible my sentence may not be confirmed. God is Good. He is all powerful and we trust in Him. Tell mother I was asking for her also Salo and the rest of the children. I will now close wishing to be remembered to all the rest.

I remain Your
Loving Son in Law
Cheerio   T Bryan [9]

B ernard Ryan wrote to his mother.

C1 Mountjoy

25/2/21

Dear Mother,

I suppose you saw the trial in the press. The counsel for the defence put up a great fight but it was to no avail.

How are all at home? I heard that you saw a couple of the boys as they [were] going for trial yesterday. We are all in the best of health and spirits. Remember me to Katie, Jack, Sarah, Agnes, Paddy, Mrs Browne, Miss Mac and all my friends. There is no news to write from in here. So Good Bye for the present.

Your fond Son

Bertie.[10]

P atrick Doyle wrote to his wife the day she gave birth to their twin daughters. In his letter he describes passing their house when being transported either to or from court and not being able to see her.[11]

Mountjoy Prison C1

Sunday 27.2.21

My Dear Louisa XXX,

I feel very anxious about you I hope you are keeping well and in good health. I wrote to you and M.E. [his sister Mary Ellen] and I got no answer yet. I know all letters are censored that may delay your letter. Dear Louisa I have been at Holy Communion this morning and I offered it up for you.

I hope and pray you may get over your illness it worry [worries] me terrible when I do think of you my Dear Louisa and I have plenty of time to think of you and my little Kathleen. I hope she is Well. I am going to ask permission from the Governor for a visit. I hope he will grant it. I would love to see you and Kathleen But I suppose you would not be able to come to see me. Please God you will recover and will be strong again. I am in great form at present. Plenty to eat and drink thanks to you. I hope Lizzie won't mind coming up with my food. I am sure it is [a] bit of a rush for you and her. I have just finish[ed] my nice Breakfast and I enjoyed it immense[ly]. We only get skilly and milk in the morning. You know how I like a cup of tea in the morning. Dear L I pass[ed] by the door twice last week but I was in a[n] armoured car. I strained my eyes to try and see you but you were not to be seen. Hard luck. I was just thinking does young Brian ever call up to see you. If he does tell him I was asking for him and his Father also T.S. I hope they are all well tell Brian to tell his Father I am a strict TT against empty bottles. I often think of the Saturday night We have to gather Drink up and have another. Just my luck. Dear Louisa we have not got our sentence yet at least not for a week or two so cheer up. I am thinking of times we are going to to have when I come Home. I would like a good dance at M.E. I am sure M.E. will give a house warmer when things brighten up a bit. I am about to write to my Mother. I will conclude with Best love to you and Kathleen also Lizzie and all down at the house.

Your loving Husband

Pat

To Kathleen   *To Louisa*

XXXXX   *XXXX*

From Daddy   *XXX*

Godbless you.

Two days later he wrote again.

Mountjoy Prison
Tuesday
C1 29.2.21

Cheer up.

My Dear Louisa XXXX Godbless you,

I received your kind and welcome letter. How glad I am to hear you are alright and your Babies. What an anxious time I have gone through, thank God, its all over and you are so Well. I am sure little Kathleen is delighted with her two dollies. I would very much like to see them and you. But I think that impossible at present. Dear Louisa I am in great form, so you need not worry about me. I hope everyone is kind to you. I know the old women and all down at [the] House looks after you. I would like to write you as my heart feels but other eyes beside your own read my letters. But dear L I am very happy. Tell my little Kathleen daddy sends her a big Love and Kisses all for herself. I suppose she misses me. Poor Kathleen I miss her. Dear Louisa I have never prayed so fervently in my life as I did for you. I say the Rosary for you every night and I know my Prayers were answered I am very thankful to the Holy Mother of God for bringing you safe. I wrote to my mother on Sunday I hope she got my letter I will write to Sarah and Fanny at least I will try. I was never a letter writer anytime. Dear Louisa I laugh when I think of the Babys one for each of us. Kathleen for me one for Lizzie and one for you. I will miss my share for a while at any rate tell Mrs Donohue I am very thankful to her for looking after you and all the kind friends who look to you in the hour of need. A friend in need is a friend indeed. I hope you are not wanting for anything. I am sure M.E. Fanny and Sarah are kind to you for my sake. Dear Louisa you can write as often as you like to me. A letter cheers me up. I am not downhearted by any means. We are a jolly lot (no complaints) all well. Tell the Mother I was expecting a letter from her and one from M.E. I think they forgot the way to write. I suppose they were busy so I will forgive them this time. I know they were attending on you. Dear Louisa I have just eaten my dinner and I enjoyed it. You are sending up what I like. You know I am not hard to please. I will conclude with best love to you and the children.

To the children God Bless you all.

XXXXX   I remain your loving husband Pat.

To Louisa   XXXX   XXXX.

Mountjoy Prison

Thursday [no date]

My Dear Louisa XXXX Godbless you.

I hope you are getting strong after your sickness. I Pray for you every night and morning. I am in the Pink. Dear Louisa you should see me scrubbing I will make an admirable husband when I come home. So cheer up don't be down hearted. I hope that my mother and all at home are well. How are all my daughters. I am the proud Father. I suppose Kathleen is jealous of her two Sisters. Poor little Kathleen I would like to see you and the three children. I hope all are kind to you. Dear Louisa what have I done, have I offended you all I got one letter since I came to this [word scribbled out by prison censor]. You know I can receive as many letters you like to write. I have no note paper or envelopes. Dear Louisa I got the book you sent in. I do read an awful lot of Books it Breaks the monotony you know. We are locked in the cell nearly all day. I seem to thrive on it I feel in great form like a two year old. I hope you will be the same when I hear from you. I['d] like to get a letter from you.

By the way M.E. never wrote to me either. Tell them all to write to me. I will conclude with Best love Kathleen, Louisa and Lizzie and all at Home Remember me to all kind friends in your trouble.

I remain your
Loving Husband
Pat
To the Children   To Louisa

XXXXXX   XXXXX

From Daddy Godbless you.

On 7 March 1921, the clerk of works of the General Prisons Board wrote to the Chairman informing him that the trapdoor in the hanghouse of Mountjoy was large enough for two executions to take place at the same time. An additional fitting could be obtained on loan from Armagh Prison at short notice if necessary.[12] There would be no problem executing the six men awaiting execution in pairs. On Friday 11 March, General Macready confirmed the four men's death sentences. Extra Auxiliaries and military were detailed to the prison. Machine guns were mounted at various points. On hearing of the decision Patrick Doyle wrote to his sister and her husband.

Friday night.   [*March 11*]
Mountjoy Prison

Dear Fanny and Barney XXX,

Just a line in answer to your welcome letter, dear sister. It's the last time I will ever write to you or Barney. Well, cheer up, I am bound for the Happy Hunting ground, on Monday. I am well prepared, so I am in great form, thank God and His Holy Mother. My only worry is my poor Louisa and our three little children. My lovely little Kathleen shall never see her Daddy again, she is young and shall soon forget. Dear Sister, be a good brave woman, don't cry, say he died for the Grand Cause, you know it was my only thought, this holy country of ours. It's worth any sacrifice, nothing too great or too big. I would gladly give twenty lives if I could. Four of us got our sentences, one got reprieved. All of us are in the best of spirits. I had the priest with me, he heard my confession, I am to receive Holy Communion in the morning, I will make general confession, so pray for me, dear sister, and brother-in-law. Remember me to all my friends. Tell Mamie [Barney's sister] I was asking for her. Good-bye Fanny and Barney. To be hanged on Monday morning at 7 o'clock.

Your loving brother Pat.

Patrick Doyle wrote his last letter to his wife.

Mountjoy Prison

My Dear Louisa XXX,

This is the last letter I shall ever write to you as I am to be ~~shot~~ hanged on Monday. I want you to be a Brave Woman for my sake and for our little children. I did not mean to give you a shock but time is so short we only got our death Sentence at 5 o'clock this evening. Please God you shall be looked after.

My Mother and ME, Fanny, Sara all will look after you for my sake. Dear Louisa my own dear Wife Pray for your Poor Pat. I know you will cheer up. I die like a soldier for a Glorious Cause. I know you will get a Shock when you read this. I want no crying or wailing of any sort be cheerful we will all be together in a very short time. Give my love to Kathleen and the other two Babies that I have never seen. You will get a visit before I am Shot. God bless you and Protect you. Remember me to Lizzie and All the Boys. Am writing to my Mother also.

To the Children	*Your Loving*
XXXXX	*Husband*
XXXXX	*Pat*
To Louisa	*XXXX XXX*

Thomas Bryan wrote to his sister Bridget.

Mountjoy Prison,

March 11th, 1921.

Dear Sister,

Just a line hoping to find you in best of health, as I am at present thank God. I know, Bridget, too well that you are much put about with regard to my case - You have heard by now, I suppose, that I am doomed to die, and that the date fixed for my execution is next Monday 14th. Well I may tell you I'm well prepared to die and am not one bit upset.

Mother was in to see me today and yesterday; she will come in everyday now. She does not mind it much, though its very hard on her I must say, but God will comfort her in her troubles. She is the best in the world. She never faltered one bit when I told her of next Monday; but she knows I'll be happy soon, and it matters very little where we die if God wills us to go.

I will not forget any of you in my prayers in the next world - you may be sure of that - and it will be a great comfort for you to know that your brother will be safe in Heaven. Don't be lonely after me, but say a wee prayer for me that God may be merciful to me. I know I will be happy anyway.

I won't forget to send some little thing to each of you in remembrance of me.

Tell all the girls I was asking for them, and I wish them a hearty good-bye.

Now Bridget be good, won't you. We shall meet in Heaven bye and bye.

From your affectionate Brother,

Tommie

XXX [13]

On 12 March, the prison began to get ready for the pending executions. D wing of Mountjoy was cleared of 56 political prisoners, and the condemned men were moved to the three condemned cells – one on each floor.[14] A series of last visits began to take place. On Saturday Patrick Moran's parish priest from Crossna visited him. He reported that Moran told him that, 'At first I didn't like the idea of being hanged for nothing, but now I am perfectly reconciled.'[15] As part of his goodbyes he signed religious cards. The one he wrote for Countess Markievicz read, 'I loved Ireland and you.'[16] Thomas Whelan had a long meeting with his mother on Saturday. Afterwards she told

Louisa Doyle with Kathleen and the surviving twin on her christening day.

the press, 'You would imagine he was going to see a football match, he was in such fine form.' He told his mother that he was completely innocent.[17] Frank Flood was visited by his father who reported that when Frank 'was informed that efforts were being made for a reprieve he replied, "We asked not for a reprieve, but for justice."'[18] Thomas Bryan was visited by his wife who was pregnant with their first child (six months later she died during childbirth). Bernard Ryan told his sister that the watchword should be, 'Carry on, no surrender.' He asked his mother and sister to 'Be brave like the women of Cork'.[19] Patrick Doyle's wife visited him on Saturday. She brought with her their three-and-a-half year old daughter and the twins. It was the first time Doyle had seen his new daughters. Tragically, on her way home from the prison one of the twins, Louisa Patricia, who had been ill, died in her mother's arms on Berkeley Road. The infant was buried in Kilbarrack on the same morning that her father was executed. Louisa Doyle told one reporter that her 'lot has been hard indeed, and I don't know why I should suffer, but this is the Lenten season, and I offer the life of my husband and child to God's holy keeping.'[20]

The Sisters of Charity wrote of their visits to the condemned men.

> The next cell visited was that occupied by P[atrick] D[oyle] and B[ernard] R[yan]. We found both men sitting before a cheery fire; they were resigned, but sad. Doyle spoke of his dear wife and twin babies and his darling little girl aged 3½. 'You would love her, Sister,' he said, 'She has lovely golden hair to her waist.'
>
> Ryan told us his widowed mother was very brave, but he was very uneasy about his delicate little sister. He was their sole support.
>
> We spoke a little about resignation to God's Holy Will and the care Divine Providence would have over those left behind. All then reverently knelt down and joined in prayer. We recited the plenary Indulgence prayer accepting whatever manner of death God wills to send us.
>
> After this the men's spirits seemed to rise and peals of laughter were heard in the cell. They said we had brought them great comfort and that they would long to see us on the morrow.
>
> We then went upstairs to the room occupied by Frank Flood and Tom Bryan. These also were a bit low spirited. Bryan spoke of his young wife whom he had loved for years, but only married lately when he was in a position to keep her. Flood was Kevin Barry's great chum. 'He sent me word that he hoped I would have a long and prosperous life, and now, here I am.'
>
> Our few words and prayers accepting God's will again did marvels here. It was with difficulty we tore ourselves away. They wanted us to talk of God. All were strong in the conviction that the fight for our country is a fight for the Faith. I am sure God will judge them according to their Faith and they may share the glory of martyrdom.
>
> On Sunday we found the men in buoyant spirits. They could not understand why God had picked them out from so many others for such a perfect preparation for death. There were no regrets, no talk

of Purgatory, but an eager longing to rush to the arms of God and to watch Ireland's cause from Heaven.

We spoke to them of our works, and asked them to help us; this they willingly agreed to do. Amongst other things, I mentioned the Foreign Missions to Whelan. 'I'll tell you what I'll do; I'll give you my little sister Annie (aged ten). When she grows up you can get her into a Foreign Mission Order.' Several times he spoke to me of Francis and Annie's budding vocations.

On Sunday he asked me if my Mother were in Heaven. I said, 'Yes', and he took messages to her and my father. He asked me to visit his mother on the day of the execution, also to correspond sometimes with her, and to inquire about Francis and Annie. This exchange of mothers reminded me of the first Good Friday.

He begged us to come back at 7 o'clock and say the Rosary for them. We got permission. That evening the prisoners' faces were radiant. Tom Bryan wrote his name on a scrap of paper and handed it to one of the nuns, saying 'When you look at that, sister, remember the joy the sisters have brought to my soul.' Before we left, Whelan, who was sitting beside me said, 'This is how I shall be tomorrow as I sit with the mother of God. Am I worthy?'

When a sister told Flood that she would pray for him from 8 to 9 o'clock on Monday, he replied, 'Why should you do that? What is to keep me out of Heaven even until 8.15?'

Playfully they talked of their places in Heaven. All seemed to agree that Whelan would be the highest. Moran was not satisfied to be away from him, and said, 'Won't you come down and stay with us, Tommy?'

Whelan was very proud of his mother. He asked one of the priests if she were as good as Kevin Barry's Mother. 'She's ten times better,' was the reply. Whelan beamed with satisfaction.

The four Dublin lads were quite satisfied with their sentence, but they bitterly resented the execution of the two innocent men, Moran and Whelan.

Priests, warders and all the other prisoners were strong in their praise of the heroic courage and fortitude of Whelan. He was at all times a great support to the others.

On Sunday, the Condemned men sang hymns all through the Mass. The warders broke down again and again. On Sunday night the doomed men slept soundly, while the guards wept over them.

All the young men were teetotallers and some of them also abstained from smoking. We noticed 2 empty porter bottles in the fireplace in Flood's cell. When he saw me looking at them he said, 'You know our friends can bring us in anything we ask for. The Black and Tan guards are decent to us, and we thought we might as well order in a drink for them.'

They organised an entertainment for the Saturday evening before their execution. Their friends brought them a supply of cakes and oranges. They met together in one of the cells and made merry. Whelan and Bryan, with their fine voices contributed musical items. Bryan also entertained the others by dressing himself up in part of the Black and Tan's uniform.

Flood casually remarked to me, 'We had been playing pitch and toss as to how we should like to die. At first I thought I would like to be shot but now I am quite indifferent.' On Tuesday we prayed over the graves of these glorious dead.

Flood desired to be buried next Kevin Barry. His request was granted. Their names are inscribed on their coffins. Let us hope that before long their remains will be removed from what was once the criminal's corner, but now is the Patriot's plot in Mountjoy Prison.[21]

A large force of Auxiliaries, with an armoured car, met the mail boat from England at Dun Laoghaire harbour. The entrance to the pier was heavily guarded and it was believed that Ellis, the hangman, was put into the armoured car and brought to Mountjoy.

On Sunday night, the eve of the executions, the men wrote their last letters.

Thomas Whelan wrote one to his parents.

13/3/21

Dear Mother and Dad,

Just a line to ask you to Pray for the Repose of my Soul. I have offered my life to God and I have no regrets. I hope I have no enemies, if I have may God Bless them. Dear Dad, if its possible do what I asked you today. I will Pray for you all when I step in to Heaven and also for all my friends which are many. When I join Piarce's[sic] Brigade I will pray for Ireland. I am sending out some things to you. Annie will have them tell May and Bridget to pray for me. Good bye now and may God Bless you all, I will pray for all. Good bye and God Bless you all.

Your solider son,
Tommy[22]

Thomas Bryan wrote to a friend.

Mountjoy Prison
13/3/21
Dublin

Cheerio & Good Luck. Blaze.

Dear George,

Just a few lines hoping to find you all at home in the Pink as this leaves me at Present, Thank God, also the folks in the Abbey, I hope your Mother has forgiven me, tell her I was asking for her. I am very glad to hear that Jim is OK again he stood my friend after my arrest.

Hell George, I won't forget you all when I go across the line, I will be able to do more than if I had lived. At 8 o'clock in the morning I go over the top and I feel assured of a good reception. It will be fine to see P.H. Pearce and the rest of the men. Well old Pal the Auxiliaries here are toffs every one and they feel it worse than we do. Remember me to all the Boys and also Miss Lynch, Mrs Smyth, Miss Flynn and Annie in Parliament St.

I am quite resigned to my fate, it is God's Holy Will and I have no regrets. It is hard on my Dear Little Wife, I know that God will give her strength to bear up as he has given me.

I don't bear any ill will against any one and hope no one bears me any, if you are writing to Lena McMahon remember me to her, also Leo and his wife.

Well dear George you have been more than a pal to me and I will remember you when I am up above. I will now Dry up with Best Wishes and the Best of Luck from your friend.

Chum.
Thomas J Bryan
P.S. Tell L.A. I will remember him when I go over the top.

Blaze.[23]

Frank Flood wrote to his sister on Friday evening having heard that his death sentence was confirmed.

Mt Joy

Friday Evg.

My dearest sister,

I know you must have heard what you may call bad news. Do not think of it as such. Think of the great grace God has given me. That might be enough to console you. I almost fear writing to Ma. I can only pray that God will console her. She must never forget that God's Will is our will.

I may see you before the appointed day but this world is so uncertain. I have hopes the governor will allowed you in if it is not forbidden by higher authorities. Everyone here have treated us very well. I do not like to praise anyone who might read this epistle, but I must say any Auxies I met here were men in the full meaning of the name.

I have no more to say except to commend myself to your pray[ers] and the prayers of all our friends.

Now sister, I must say goodbye or perhaps not Goodbye but Aur Revoir for in a few years we will meet in heaven.

Farewell and may God bless and protect you till we meet in heaven.

Your fond brother

Frank.[24]

The night before he was executed Frank Flood wrote to his sister.

Sunday Evening
13th March

Dear Allie,

Just a line of Goodbye before leaving for Heaven. There must be no weeping after me. I am going where I might never have reach[ed] if I lived my ordinary life. Tomorrow I will be in heaven and praying for you all who must remain here below after us.

Now goodbye and God bless and protect you until we meet in heaven.

Again goodbye and always remember me as a true and fond brother and a Soldier of Ireland.

Yours truly, Frank.[25]

Flood then wrote letters to his friend Frank Carberry and his brother Sean.

Dear Frank,

We are going to heaven tomorrow or to use our Kevin's [Barry] phrase we are going 'over the top'. So Cheer up and do not act the silly kipper. Goodbye and God bless you And keep you from all danger. I will watch over the fight. Goodbye and think of your old friend and Comrade.

Frank

It is after one o'clock and I am going to bed so tell all the boys I could not write them all. But I remember them all.[26]

Sunday night

13th March

My dear Brother Sean,

Goodbye and good luck and long life in the cause. My only regret is to have done so little for Ireland, but this is outweighed by the thought of how much we can do in heaven for Ireland in the great fight. Goodbye again and may God bless and protect you from all dangers until heaven is your reward. Think of me as your brother who did his duty to the best of his ability and failed through God's will. I am your fond brother.

Frank [27]

The next morning the *Freeman's Journal* reported on the scene outside the prison.

Freeman's Journal March 14 1921

OUTSIDE THE JAIL GATES
Sorrowful Crowds Offer Prayers for Prisoners

SIGNALS PASS

Demonstration by girls of
The Cumann na mBan

Last evening large crowds gathered around Mountjoy Prison.

The subdued demeanour of the people, their anxious looks, and whispered talk, were all indicative of the mingled feelings of sympathy and horror in which they regarded the awful tragedy at hand.

When the dusk approached the scene became so impressive as to stir the dullest imagination and warm the coldest heart.

As the last light of expiring day died down behind the grim towers of Mountjoy its cruel walls stood forth in black relief, and in the calmness of the evening air the big flag over the prison lay limp and lifeless on the flagstaff.

PRAYERS IN THE STREET

Then the voices of the multitude in prayer again rang out in the solemn stillness of the evening. It was a wonderful gathering of Irishmen and women of every rank and station united by the single thought of knocking at Heaven's gate for their brave young countrymen who would ere long stand before the Judgement Seat.

And if they thought of mortal things at all their only prayer was that God would still strengthen the spirit of the brave and in the last mortal struggle sustain them.

At the conclusion of the Rosary, about 6 o'clock, there was a thrilling little scene. With the passing of daylight the crowd observed lights in a number of windows situated in the north wing. They were flickering lights, like those of fires in the cells of the doomed men.

SIGNALS WAVED

One man claimed that he saw a signal, and a great many people waved handkerchiefs. There was no response for 15 minutes. Then quite clearly a hand came to one of the windows and waved a large white handkerchief again and again. With a great surge of joy the crowd waved hats and handkerchiefs. And in an instant all was silent and lifeless again.

Before dispersing, towards Curfew hour last night the crowds outside Mountjoy Prison sang 'The Soldiers Song' and 'Wrap the Green Flag Around Me, Boys.'

In the Catholic churches in the city yesterday the celebrants of the Masses asked for the prayers of the congregation for the spiritual welfare of their countrymen about to be executed.

Ten o'clock Mass at Booterstown Church was offered up yesterday for Patrick Moran and the 8 o'clock Mass this (Monday) morning will also be offered up for him. Masses and prayers for the condemned man were also offered in Blackrock, where he was well known and where belief in his innocence is general.

DEMONSTRATION BY WOMEN

Procession of the Cumann na mBan Girls

Several hundred members of Cumann-na-mBan walked in procession yesterday from Stephen's Green through some of the principal streets of Dublin to Mountjoy Prison.

They carried two large and two small Banners bearing in large letters the words, 'England executes prisoners of war,' 'They murder the innocent in vengeance,' and 'Join with us in protest.'

The demonstration attracted considerable attention. [The article continues.]

Left: Mrs Whelan, centre, with shawl, and Maud Gonne on right.
Right: religious picture being attached to prison gate on morning of 14 March 1921.

Freeman's Journal, 14 March 1921

SIX IRISHMEN DIE TO-DAY

ALL HOPE OF REPRIEVE OF MOUNTJOY PRISONERS ABANDONED LAST EVENING

TO BE HANGED IN THREE BATCHES

Pathetic Incidents Yesterday: Parents Take Leave of their Doomed Sons in Jail

All hope of reprieve for the six young men lying under sentence of death in Mountjoy Jail was abandoned last evening, and by the time this issue is in the hands of readers six more young lives will have been sacrificed for Ireland, unless at the last moment the prerogative of mercy is exercised.

Some of the prisoners are mere boys; two are but 19 years of age. Four of them were sentenced to death on charges of taking part in an ambush at Clonturk Park, Drumcondra, and the others were sentenced in connection with the shootings on Sunday, Nov. 21.

The news that their lives were to be forfeited caused a shock throughout Ireland, and strong hopes were entertained that they would be reprieved. These were finally dispelled last evening, when the Lord Mayor was officially informed that there was no hope for the men. It is understood that they will be exected in batches of two, the first at 6 o'clock this morning, the second at 7, and the last two at 8. The parents and relatives of the doomed men visited them in prison for the last time yesterday.

The National Executive of the Irish Labour Party yesterday issued a call to the workers of Dublin to abstain from labour till 11 o'clock to-day, and to observe the morning as a period of mourning and solemn protest.

At 5.20 a.m Canon Waters celebrated Mass for Whelan and Moran. It was celebrated in their cell in which a small altar had been erected. The two embraced before they were hanged at 6 o'clock. According to the hangman's report Whelan was dropped seven feet five inches and Moran seven feet eight inches. Their bodies were immediately anointed. Next came Doyle and Ryan. Canon Waters heard their confessions and Father MacMahon said Mass for them (a Black and Tan took Holy Communion with them). When the executioner entered 'they stood up, not perturbed'. Doyle was given a drop of seven feet ten inches and Ryan a drop of eight feet one inch. The last pair to meet their end that morning was Frank Flood and Thomas Bryan. It is impossible to know what went through the men's minds when the clock ticked down their final hours. However, Flood and Bryan were apparently so relaxed that at 7.20 they needed to be woken for their own deaths. They had slept soundly. Brought downstairs to the ground-floor cell where the altar had been set up, the two knelt and prayed and 'tears gathered in the eyes of the priests and warders and Auxiliaries that were present'. Bryan fell eight feet ten inches and Flood seven feet one inch.[28]

The following day the press described the scene outside the prison.

Freeman's Journal, 14 March 1921

THE VIGIL AT DAWN
How the Watchers Waited Outside Mountjoy Jail

COURAGE AND PRAYER

'They have done it!' cried a spectator passionately when a characteristically worded official notice appeared on the jail gate to announce that six more brave men had died for Ireland. The surprise and passion epitomised the scene. There was a death-bed stillness around the prison. No bell had tolled to tell us there was one man less in Ireland. Five thousand Dublin citizens had kept a proud and devoted vigil that had commenced at dawn. In twos and threes students, young girls, labourers hastened through the still lighted streets. Outside Mountjoy the dim khaki patrols glided up and down. An armoured car wandered along the street amongst the slowly growing crowd, barely fifty strong at first. On the damp pavement the small group knelt and prayed aloud.

Praying In The Dawn

'God and His Holy Mother give glory to poor Ireland!' cried a woman's voice as the Rosary finished. The sky cleared. The police on guard outside the iron gates retired within. The armoured car glided through the swelling crowds. Two youths climbed up on the outer wall. They lighted candles and a lamp before the statues of the Sacred Heart and Blessed Virgin. Through the crowds women held lighted candles in their hands. Here and there one heard a stifled sob, or a woman moved away with pallid face and agonised eyes. The silent khaki sentries seemed turned to marble, and the huge crowd prayed for the men who were soon to die.

Every ear was strained for the bell which never tolled. Six struck from distant churches. Patrick Moran and Thomas Whelan were dead, but nothing more than an intenser note in the prayers indicated the sacrifice. The military withdrew at 6.30 and the outer gates of Mountjoy were opened. The watchers swept in like a tide before the prison. Children swarmed up to adjacent railings or the bleak and dripping trees.

The Girl With The Crucifix

Until seven o'clock the Rosary was recited and hymns were sung. A young girl held a crucifix above the reverent populace before the jail gate. 'We will be true to Thee till death!' a thousand voices echoed and thrilled. At 7 Thomas Ryan and Patrick Doyle passed like their gallant comrades untolled. Here and there the emotions of the crowd found relief in short exclamations.

'God have mercy on them.' 'It's an old story.' 'Of course they are innocent.' The crucifix was still held above the throng as 8 o'clock struck, and the sacrifice was completed. And again the words thrilled and echoed – 'We will be true to Thee till death!' And yet it was hard to realise that six Irishmen had been hanged. All classes of Dublin people were there, from newsboy to merchant, from peasant to priest, from young girls to aged women; subdued, calm, undaunted before the mute granite temple of death.

The Notice on the Gate

Twenty past eight, and the tension was broken. The jail gate swung half open, a small white notice was nailed up, something half a hiss and half a sigh passed through the weary ranks. The Rosary was again recited for the repose of the dead men's souls. The crowds slowly dispersed into the thronged streets, through which already passed a solitary lorry menacing, with levelled rifle, or revolver. And in the faces of Dublin's men and women, returning from that poignant vigil, there gleamed an austere and pensive pride. The souls of six young Irishmen had passed into heaven, and their heritage into the keeping of their people.

Part of the large crowd outside Mountjoy on the morning of 14 March 1921.

After the executions each of the families immediately put in requests for the bodies of their loved ones to be returned for burial outside the prison. Thomas Whelan's mother wrote:

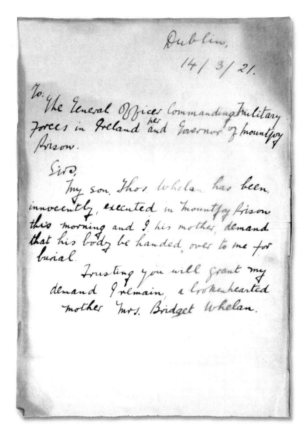

Dublin

14/3/21

To:

The General Officer Commanding Military Forces in Ireland and her Governor of Mountjoy Prison.

Sirs,

My son, Thos Whelan has been, innocently, executed in Mountjoy Prison this morning and I, his mother, demand that his body be handed over to me for burial.

Trusting you will grant my demand I remain, a broken hearted mother, Mrs. Bridget Whelan.[29]

The requests were refused and the bodies were buried in a common grave in the same part of the prison where Kevin Barry had been buried the previous November.

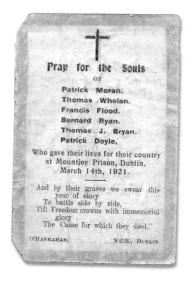

17–3–20 [sic]

To the Governor
Mountjoy Prison

From John Flood
20 Summerhill Parade

Please send to the above address a certificate of the death of Francis X Flood of same address.[30]

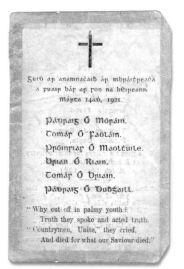

Notes to the text

1. Piaras Beaslai, *Michael Collins and the Making of a New Ireland*, Vol. II, Phoenix, London, 1926, pp. 157-8.

2. See *Irish Times,* 1-22 January 1921.

3. Courtesy of Ryan family.

4. Courtesy of Bryan family.

5. Courtesy of Ryan family.

6. Public Record Office (PRO), War Office (WO) 71/364.

7. Ibid.

8. Courtesy of Doyle family.

9. Kilmainham Goal and Museum.

10. Courtesy of Ryan family.

11. All Patrick Doyle's letters courtesy of the Doyle family.

12. General Prison Board (GPB) 1921, 2165.

13. Kilmainham Goal and Museum.

14. GPB 1921, 2169.

15. *Irish Independent*, 14 March 1921.

16. Kilmainham Goal and Museum.

17. *Irish Independent*, 14 March 1921.

18. *Freeman's Journal*, 15 March 1921.

19. *Freeman's Journal*, 14 March 1921.

20. *Irish Independent*, 15 March 1921.

21. National Library of Ireland, MS Accession number 5140.

22. *Freeman's Journal*, 15 March 1921.

23. Kilmainham Goal and Museum.

24. Courtesy of Fr. Fergal MacDonagh.

25. Courtesy of Fr. Fergal MacDonagh.

26. Kilmainham Goal and Museum.

27. Kilmainham Goal and Museum.

28. GPB 1921, 2169.

29. GPB 1921, 2221.

30. GPB 1921, 2418.

4

Thomas Traynor, Edmond Foley
& Patrick Maher

ATTACK AT BRUNSWICK STREET, 14 MARCH 1921

As the city of Dublin was coming to terms with the six executions that took place in Mountjoy prison on the morning of 14 March, one of the largest gun battles to have taken place in the city occurred on Brunswick Street (now Pearse Street). A Rolls Royce armoured car and two lorries of Auxiliaries had left Dublin Castle to raid 144 Brunswick Street. This house was the headquarters of the Dublin Brigade of the IRA. When the lorries arrived for the raid, IRA men who were patrolling the area around number 144 attacked them from a number of directions. In the ensuing firefight there were a number of casualties. Two men were captured. One had been wounded and subsequently died. The other was Thomas Traynor. In just over a month Traynor would be buried in the Patriots' Plot in Mountjoy prison. The next day the *Freeman's Journal* reported on the attack.

Freeman's Journal, 15 March 1921

THREE MEN SHOT DEAD
Desperate Shooting Affray in Dublin Ends in Many Casualties
Mysterious Bomb Explosion

Five Auxiliary Cadets and Three Civilians Wounded in Reported Attack

Three civilians were killed, three wounded, and five Auxiliary cadets were injured – two seriously – in the course of a desperate shooting affray which occurred in Great Brunswick Street, Dublin, at about 8.15 last night.

Shortly before these tragedies, which occurred near Westland Row, a bomb exploded near the Central Police Station [now Pearse Street Garda station], nearly half a mile away, and a civilian received injuries which necessitated the amputation of a leg.

A report from Military Headquarters states that the Auxiliaries were attacked as they were about to raid a house, and that they returned the fire of their assailants.

People in the vicinity were terrified, and took refuge in shops and doorways. They state that for some time they heard sporadic outbursts of shooting, including machine-gun fire.

Startled Pedestrians Take Cover

Shortly before 8 o'clock last night a terrific explosion was heard in Great Brunswick street, outside the Central Police Station.

A military lorry arrived on the scene almost immediately and a civilian was taken to Mercer's Hospital seriously injured in the leg.

Civilians and tramcars were subsequently held up and searched by Crown forces. About 8.15 firing was heard near Westland Row, followed by a terrified stampede of pedestrians.

According to one account, a lorry-load of Auxiliaries was attacked and returned the fire.

Conflicting reports of both occurrences were current. One account was to the effect that a bomb was dropped near a lower window of the police station. A loud explosion followed, and several panes of glass were broken, but wire netting on the window prevented more extensive damage.

CIVILIANS LEG AMPUTATED

A civilian passing at the time sustained serious injury, which afterwards necessitated amputation of the leg.

About 15 minutes later, according to same version, a lorry load of Auxiliaries was ambushed between Brunswick St. Library and Westland Row railway station. A bystander told a *Freeman's Journal*

representative that he heard several loud explosions, followed by rifle fire, while standing at the entrance to Westland Row railway station. D.M.P. constables on duty warned pedestrians to take cover. Almost immediately a lorry rushed past.

A semi-official version of the incidents states that shortly after 8 o'clock a man dropped a bomb in the middle of Great Brunswick Street opposite College Street police station. The bomb exploded, blew his leg off, and broke some of the windows in the station.

A few minutes later Auxiliaries, who were in the same thoroughfare, were attacked with bombs and revolvers. They returned the fire, wounding one man, whom they captured. The officer in charge took a second man prisoner.

After his arrest it was alleged that Traynor had been badly beaten in Dublin Castle by members of the 'Igoe gang' of Auxiliaries. Unlike the other men hanged in Mountjoy, the time between Thomas Traynor's capture and his court martial was relatively short – just over three weeks. At City Hall on 4 April 1921, he was court-martialled on the charge that he 'on the 14th March, 1921, feloniously, wilfully and of his malice aforethought, did kill and murder Francis Joseph Farrell'. Traynor faced the President of the Court, Major F.S. Montague Bates and the jury made up of Lieutenant Colonel E.H. Chapman, OBE, Major E.L. Makin, Major A.W. Langley, Captain A.G.M. Sharpe and Captain H.G. Moor Gwynn. At the outset of the trial Thomas Traynor's defence counsel strongly

Captain Igoe of the Auxiliaries.

protested that the same President of the court martial in Patrick Moran's trial would sit in charge of Traynor's court. The counsel stated that had he and his client been given proper notice of the members of the court they would have objected to a person they felt was biased. [1] For the purpose of the court martial Traynor was treated as if he were a member of the First Battalion of the Lancashire Fusiliers, Ship Street Barracks, Dublin.

Thomas Traynor was born in 1882 in Tullow, County Carlow; he was one of ten children. He moved to Dublin when he was about 18 and learned his trade as a shoemaker. Strongly involved in the nationalist movement he fought in Boland's Mills under de Valera in 1916. Afterwards he was interned in Frongoch Camp in North Wales where the internee's General Council appointed him master-shoemaker for the camp.[2] In 1917 he was released in the general amnesty which saw the release of all internees. When he returned to Dublin he lived at 142 McCaffrey Street, Mount

Thomas Traynor.

Brown, and his shoe shop was near Crown Alley. At this time he was attached to B Company of the 3rd Battalion of the Dublin Brigade. While Kevin Barry represented youth, promise and a future cut short, Traynor was of an older generation. In 1921 he was 39 years old and was married. He had met his wife Elizabeth while walking around St Stephen's Green in Dublin; because she was a Protestant the two had eloped. They had ten children. At the time of Traynor's execution the eldest was 18, the youngest just five months.

Mountjoy Prison

T. Traynor

Dear Lizzie,

Just a line to let you know where I am. I was brought here on Tuesday. I want you to let me know at once how you are, there is some money that I had in my pocket here if you see the Governor of the prison you will get it. Send me in some cigarettes, matches, comb, hat, the food here is not what I was used to you might send in a couple of cooked sausages and eggs and also some sugar.

Tell Fran and Tommy to get the best the[y] can with the work and if the[y] want to know anything, you can write in to me.

Write as soon as possible

Love to all

Tom.[3]

In his statement Traynor told the court that he had never been asked to take an active part in the current conflict. However, since he was a long-standing republican and a member of the republican movement he would have been a person who could have been entrusted with a message. The pistol he was found carrying had been dropped in to his workshop on the Monday with the words, 'Bring this to No. 144 Gt. Brunswick Street about 8 o'clock, and you will find someone there to take it from you.' When Traynor arrived at the address at around 8.10 military lorries stopped beside him and were attacked. At that point he took the gun out of his pocket and ran down the street. He was captured and put into an armoured car and covered with revolvers.

During the case the main argument of the defence centred on the fact that there was no evidence that Traynor had fired the gun in his possession. It was an unfortunate coincidence that he arrived just as the attack took place. On the other hand the prosecution argued that the fact that Traynor was at the site of the ambush and was armed was sufficient reason to convict him, by association, of the murder of Cadet Farrell. Towards the end of the court martial the defence counsel argued, although he admitted that he was not permitted to put up such a defence, that Traynor was a soldier caught in a battle between two belligerent forces. According to the rules of warfare it was unjust to execute a soldier captured in the course of a battle.

CLOSING STATEMENT FOR THE DEFENCE *[Underlining as in the original manuscript]*

Mr Whelan:

The statement of the Accused, I submit to you, is true in fact. There may be many matters that one would like to have asked but unfortunately in this country, as distinct from England, it is not possible, it is against the law, to swear the Accused and to put him into the box where he can be examined by his own counsel and cross-examined by the counsel for the Prosecution and have any other matters cleared up by the learned Judge Advocate or Members of the Court... He says he was a member of the movement: 'I was in the movement in 1916.' You are all aware of the fact, it is a matter of public knowledge, of what took place at the Easter of 1916. He also says: 'I have never yet been asked by the Republican Party to take any active part in the present activity.' In other words really the interpretation of that is, that he was a Member of the Irish Republican Party, that is what the reference to 1916 is, and he <u>was out in Easter Week of 1916 fighting</u>. That is what I suggest is the meaning of his statement that he made, that he is still a member of that Republican Party, and apparently, as a member of the Irish Republican Army, would come out and fight if called upon, but that has not yet been called upon to do so. The reason, I suggest, for his not being called upon to fight, is because, as he tells you, he is a boot maker; he has a small business in the City assisted by his two boys, and he has a wife and 10 children. <u>It is a matter of public knowledge</u>

<u>that the Irish Republican Army have a considerable number of men at their disposal operating in different parts of Ireland, and it is a matter of common knowledge, and I think it is a very fair assumption to come to, that the time has not yet come for them to call upon married men with a wife and 10 children.</u> His explanation is that, having been out in 1916, he would be a trustworthy reliable person to carry a revolver and deliver it to 144 Great Brunswick Street... He was going out, if his statement is correct, to deliver this revolver to some of the gunmen in ignorance of anything that would happen or that would be likely to happen there. If his statement is correct he went down there, and just about the time that this convoy arrived he, unfortunately for himself, happened to be there. The firing started, but, as you were told, or rather, as the evidence, I submit, proves, all this attack was made by different groups from different portions of that Area. You had one group at one corner of Sandwith Street with a retreat open to it; you have another group on the opposite corner of Sandwith Street with a retreat open to it, and you had a further group, as I shall call them, in the house, no. 144, with a retreat apparently open also, and in the house 145 with a retreat open to it; also you were told that there was firing from the far side of the street, that would be the left hand side, with a retreat apparently open, but there is no evidence before you that there was any isolated people on that footpath firing – isolated individuals – that is between 144 and the beginning of Sandwith Street. There is no evidence of that, and if his statement is correct, he just happened to be on the footpath there and I think put his back to the railings when the firing took place. You were told that the mode in which the attackers were located – it was a very dark night – the mode in which they were located was by the flashes of the revolvers or the automatics, whichever they were using. If this man was firing and he was up against the railings the flashes of his automatic would have been seen by somebody in the tenders or the armoured car, they being quite close to the footpath, and he would have been shot dead or, at least,

very badly wounded; but there was no evidence of any wounding, and they took him unwounded, which, I submit, would be an impossibility if he had been firing as he would have been located by the flashes. His story is that he stayed there and: 'When the firing ceased a little I took the thing out of my pocket and ran back towards Sandwith Street', in other words, as soon as there was a little lull in the firing, which you were told by two or three witnesses took place two or three minutes after the outburst... he ran away as soon as there was a lull in the firing. That is consistent with the evidence, and so far all the evidence given bears out in toto the statement of the Accused...

With regard to the statement made by the accused when he was on the ground, a witness has told you that he was not quite sure of the exact words, but that he said, 'Shoot me now' or something to that effect. He was not sure of the exact words, but 'Shoot me and put an end to it now', and that witness admitted he may have said something like 'Do me in now.' I submit the accused being on his back on the ground, with a knee on his chest, and a grip on his hand, and another officer there with a revolver, that he was frightened, and when he said 'Do me in now; do me in now', I suggest that it would be better to be done then than at any other time, but it is in no way contrary to his evidence at all. This automatic discharges its bullets as they are fired. You have the bullet in front of you, and it has got some marks upon it. I will ask you to inspect that bullet, and if the accused fired any shots, the case of the bullet would be at some place on the footpath, and I think it is a reasonable suggestion that if any cases corresponding to them had been found, they would have been produced here, because the prosecution have all the resources at their command, and I submit it is the duty of the authorities to have searched that place and find out what cartridges or dead bullets there were... there is no empty case produced which corresponds to the particular design of those found in the automatic in the pockets of the accused. The automatic itself appeared to me, in the first instance, to be very stiff, and not to be working very easily, and on the second occasion when the clip went in the court saw the difficulty there was in getting it out, and I would ask you to say the automatic was not in a satisfactory manner for use and that it was given to the prisoner to bring along to someone else who would probably get it repaired... You will have no sympathy I am sure with the members of the Irish Republican Army, and he has undoubtedly prejudiced himself by telling you, as I read his statement, that he is and was a member of the Irish Republican Army, but that only goes to show the truth of his statement. If I am correct in interpreting his remarks that he is a member of the Irish Republican Army, it is not open to him to produce any evidence, because anybody who came here to produce it would be tried possibly upon a similar charge, or upon some other charge of a serious nature. For instance the people who were in that house or in that attack, none of them could be produced to tell you that the accused was not a participator, none of them, and I do suggest that the person who handed him the revolver could not possibly be produced, and the result is that it is impossible in the circumstances to produce evidence for the defence on this line of defence that I am making for the accused. If you believe the statement of the accused, being a military tribunal unconsciously it may affect you, but if you believe his statement he will be acquitted, and let at large, and you may think he will be out in arms against one of yourselves in the near future; that unconsciously may affect you, but we know as a matter of common knowledge that if you do release him, he would be arrested immediately and interned, so that he is not at the moment a danger to any of the armed forces of the Crown. It is an unfortunate coincidence, if the statement is correct, that he happened just to have arrived at the moment the armoured car came on the scene, but in the present state of things in Dublin it is an unfortunate coincidence, as you will know, for many innocent people to be caught in a place like that, but owing to the existing state of affairs it is an occurrence which might occur to any one of you tomorrow. What was suggested in the opening statement of the learned counsel for the prosecution was that possibly you might come to the conclusion that he was a scout, an outpost watching; if he was he would have seen the cars coming, and he would naturally have joined up with some of the groups operating on that occasion.

The onus of proof lies upon the Crown, and if you have any reasonable doubt of any sort or description as to whether the statement made by the accused is accurate or not, you must give that doubt to the prisoner. The charge is one of murder; a man's life is at stake, and in a charge of that nature the case must be proved beyond all reasonable doubt... Well, in this case I submit to you it would be very much less certain that the accused participated in this encounter than in many other cases where the court directed there was a reasonable doubt and had to give it in favour of the accused. It is right for me to point out that although the charge here is murder, and that is the only charge before you, in a case of murder it is open to the court to bring in a verdict of manslaughter. There is no evidence before you of participation. He was in no way attached to any group, and there is no evidence he shot anybody. There is no evidence that the revolver was fired during the conflict. He was solitary. He was not amongst any group of men, and I submit that there is no evidence of his aiding, abetting or in any way being a participant in the conflict that took place.

Now the other branch, if you do not come to the conclusion that the accused's statement is correct, or alternatively you think the case for the prosecution has been made out, the alternative defence I was putting up was that it was a conflict between forces of the British Army and the forces of the Irish Republican Army, but I have been debarred from making this point as I have not the evidence to prove to you that there is a state of war. If you will assume that there is a state of war, or if it is granted that there was a state of war in existence, I would be in a position to argue that he, <u>as a prisoner of war, could not be tried for murder, because in war it is not murder to shoot, and</u>

the charge would fall. In olden times war or rebellion was confined in isolated districts, but with the development of transport, with the development of science, the area has extended, until during the last war it extended over a very large portion of Europe. Civilisation in its development laid down certain rules of war; prior to that prisoners were shot, atrocities perpetrated on women, and various other matters like that... England I believe boasts that she led the way for civilisation, and she showed the light to the world in civilisation, and was party to the rules of war to which I have referred. They were gradually developed. What for? As I say to protect humanity and develop civilisation, but what difference is there with regard to civilisation and humanity I am talking now, and I press this point upon you, what difference is there with regards humanity, whether the fighting is between two self-distinct and independent powers or between the armed forces of the English Government on the one part and the armed forces of the Irish Republic on the other? With regard to humanity and civilisation I suggest there is no difference whatever as long as the combat is carried out between civilised people. It is not in the least between people within the country, it is between one country and another country... I submit on the evidence you must come to the conclusion that this took place in a conflict between the armed forces of the Irish Republic and the armed forces of the Crown, and that you also will realise as a matter of common knowledge that a state of war exists in the greater part of Ireland. If my contention is correct, if you think the case for the prosecution has been proved with regard to his aiding, abetting and participating, the accused then is a prisoner, and as such a charge of murder does not lie against him. My learned friend, in replying, will possibly quote to you the law telling you that rebels are not to be entitled to the rules of war, and possibly quote you authorities, but you must recollect that it is a matter of common knowledge that the British Constitution is only partly written, and partly unwritten. The laws are likewise only partly statutory and partly common law, and as time has developed so have the unwritten laws developed, and I suggest to you that in the present condition of civilisation the shooting of rebels is contrary to them, and it is not open to you to bring in a verdict of murder against the accused.

The Counsel for the prosecution countered the argument of the defence.

You will remember... that the case, as opened to you, was that this man was taking part in an attack during which a murder was committed. If my friend is right and that this was, as I understand his submission to be, a battle between two properly recognised forces, officially recognised, and recognised internationally, and recognised from every point of view, that would not be murder, but that this man would be allowed to take part in an attack of this kind and if people were killed as a result of it it would not be murder... Now, is there the slightest justification for the proposition that my friend contends here... it would be idle for me to labour the point that this force, the Irish Republican Army, as I understand it is called, has ever been recognised by His Majesty's Government in England – recognised to hold the position of a belligerent force carrying on war against them in the sense that war has been carried on before by belligerent nations and belligerent countries throughout history; and is that surprising when you, Sir, and every Member of the Court knows the nature of warfare, the nature of the belligerency that is carried on by this so-called Irish Republican Army; men, civilians one moment, and the next nothing short of murderers; men who are amenable to no kind of organisation or discipline such has been laid down over and over again and, as you know, is especially referred to in the Schedule to the Hague Convention...'(1) They must be commanded by a person responsible for his subordinates; (2) They must have a fixed distinctive sign recognizable at a distance; (3) They must carry arms openly; and (4) They must conduct their operations in accordance with the laws and customs of war.' Is there one of those 4 precepts carried out today in Ireland or was carried out, which is perhaps more to the point, on the fatal day, the 14th March in the street...

This man on the spot with an automatic pistol in the most dangerous possible state at a time when automatic pistols are being fired by men who we know now are members of the same movement to which this man belonged, who, though according to my friend is too old, is not too old to run and not too old to be there in the middle of the fight. I submit there can only be one Finding in this case, that this man was there not a member of a belligerent party fighting another properly recognised belligerent party, but was a member of a rebel gang, a civilian in plain clothes who could be turned in one moment from that civilian status to a most dangerous member of society whom it is the duty of the Crown Forces, as best they can, to contend with and put down. So far from being entitled to the privileges of a prisoner of war if the Court thinks that that is so, the sentence which may or may not be passed upon him is a just one and one which I do not hesitate to say he richly deserves.[4]

On Thursday 21 April, Traynor was informed that his death sentence had been confirmed by General Macready. Dublin Castle issued the following statement to the press.

> Orders have been given that Thomas Traynor, who was convicted by courtmartial on the 5th inst. of the murder of Temporary Cadet Farrell, of the Auxiliary Division, RIC, in Brunswick street, is to be executed.

> On the night of the murder, at about 8 p.m., two tenders containing Auxiliaries and an armoured car drove up Brunswick street and stopped outside No. 144. Just as they were stopping, fire was opened upon them from all sides, and Temporary Cadet Farrell, who was sitting in the leading tender, fell mortally wounded.

The night was dark, and that the ambush was a prepared one was shown by the fact that the street lamp immediately outside No. 144 had been extinguished. The Auxiliaries could only fire at the flashes from their assailants' revolvers.

Heavy firing continued for six or seven minutes, and during a lull an officer, seated at the rear of the armoured car, saw a civilian run past him. He fired his last shot at him and then sprang from the car, chased him, and brought him down with a Rugby tackle, at the same time calling another officer to his assistance. The prisoner was Traynor, and he had in his hand a German automatic, with four cartridges in the magazine and one in the breech, and a clip of six cartridges in his pocket.

After the firing ceased it was found that the Section Leader was so seriously wounded that he subsequently died from his wounds. Three civilians were found dead, one of whom had in his hand a five-chambered revolver, and another was clutching a bag containing 130 rounds of revolver ammunition.

Temporary Cadet Farrell was an Irishman, born in Dublin. He was 28 years of age, and had served with distinction in the war, being once wounded and mentioned in despatches. At the time of the armistice he was Adjutant of his battalion.

Section Leader Beard enlisted at the outbreak of the war, and rose rapidly until at the time of the armistice he was Acting Brigade Major of the 54th Infantry Brigade. He was awarded the Military Cross.[5]

The countdown to Traynor's execution began. D wing was cleared of prisoners and he was transferred to the condemned cell on the ground floor. A number of people and organisations called for a reprieve. These included the Archbishop of Cashel and the Irish Transport Union who called on the outgoing Viceroy, Lord French, for 'a last act of clemency'. According to sources in Dublin Castle there was no hope of a reprieve. On Sunday a Dublin Castle source was quoted as saying 'there can be no postponement'.[6] Traynor received his final visits. On Sunday over 90 people visited him. His brother was reported to have said, 'He laughed and talked as freely as if he were sitting in the shop attending his trade.' When his family said goodbye to him for the last time he stood outside the cell and saluted them. His wife was the last to leave. On his last night as he smoked a cigarette he blew smoke-rings. Turning to one of his guards he said, 'Imagine, one of those will be around my neck tomorrow.' The next day the press reported on the eighth execution in Mountjoy Prison in six months.

Elizabeth Traynor and child outside Mountjoy Prison the morning of the execution.

Freeman's Journal, 26 April 1921

ANOTHER IRISH MARTYR

THOMAS TRAYNOR WALKS TO THE SCAFFOLD CALMLY AND WITH HEAD ERECT

SCENES OUTSIDE MOUNTJOY

Early Morning Vigil: Crowds Pray Fervently: Aged Mother's Pride in Brave Son

Another Irishman made the supreme sacrifice in Mountjoy Jail yesterday morning.

Thomas Traynor, the father of ten children, most of them little ones, and some mere babes, walked to the scaffold unfalteringly with head erect.

Sentenced by courtmartial in connection with the Brunswick street ambush, he willingly offered his life in the cause of Ireland, and went to his death reconciled to his God and with a prayer on his lips, dying, as he lived, a devout Catholic.

Impressive scenes were witnessed outside the jail in the early morning, large crowds, including the widow and other relatives, fervently praying for spiritual comfort, and, when the fatal hour of 8 had struck, for the repose of the soul of the brave man.

As a prison warder was about to affix to the jail gates the notice of the execution, it was torn from his hand by the indignant people assembled outside.

An application by a solicitor on behalf of the widow, claiming the body, was not acceded to, and the remains were interred within the jail walls, side by side with Kevin Barry and the six other brave young men recently executed.

LAST DAYS AND FINAL MOMENTS

From an early hour in the morning large crowds began to gather under the frowning walls of Mountjoy Prison, and soon the welling chorus of their prayers arose in supplication to Heaven for Ireland's latest martyr.

Before 7 o'clock the first batches of pilgrims began to arrive and take up their positions around the prison entrance. Men and women, young and old, rich and poor – people of every rank and station came on that early vigil to pray in common for strength and consolation for the condemned man in the hour of his trial. Amongst a few on the outskirts of the crowd there was indeed a little hushed and quiet gossip of reprieve, but the bulk of the people gave it no thought, and turned their hearts and souls entirely to prayer.

The Rosary in Irish, recited by the Cumann na mBan, was followed by the singing of 'Hail, Queen of Heaven,' in which all the people joined till the strains of the hymn rose triumphantly in the morning air.

Executions Recalled

Memories of Kevin Barry, the Boy Martyr

The scene in its sorrow and impressiveness recalled those other mornings outside Mountjoy when Kevin Barry, the boy hero, died, and when the glorious six calmly faced the cold embrace of death that Ireland might live. Yesterday morning it was no youth whose bright spirit was to be quenched, it was no young man in the first flush of life's hope and strength that had to make the supreme sacrifice, but a man of riper years, the responsible head of a family, and the father of ten children, most of them little ones, and some mere babes. Yet in their sympathy there was no weakness, but rather a note of pride in the unbending courage of those Irishmen who have faced death and danger for freedom's sake.

The Fatal Hour

As the hour of eight approached the sun shone out gloriously, and with its golden shafts brightly gilded the grim towers of Mountjoy and their encircling walls.

All within the prison seemed as silent as the grave, and from that vast tomb-like place came no sign or token as the hour of eight approached.

The shrill scream of a steam siren in the distance was the first herald that the fatal hour had struck. The prayers for spiritual comfort now became prayers for the repose of a gallant soul, and ere they died away the prison made its first sign. The wicket gate in the main door was slightly opened and the arm of a warder stretched forth with the brief official notice that 'the sentence of the law' had been carried out. For the first time at scenes of this character a burst of indignation arose from the assembled people. The notice was never tacked to the door; it was literally torn from the warder's hand. But in a flash the storm was over, and a woman's voice rang out: 'May the Lord have mercy on that man's soul.' Responses of 'Amen' and prayers again arose, mingled with loud sobbing of the little boy, one of the executed man's sons. He was helped away, weeping bitterly.

Widow's Terrible Ordeal

Relatives Bearing Their Cross With Great Fortitude

Mrs. Traynor, the widow, who had spent all the morning at the jail gate, collapsed and lay for a few minutes limp and lifeless in the arms of her friends. Around her stood her other relatives, now that the tension was over, bathed in tears. She was soon taken to a cab and escorted by kind friends from the scene of her husband's sacrifice and of her own great trial and sorrow. In a few minutes the crowd had broken up and dispersed, but not without eager efforts on all sides to secure one of the candles as a memento to yet another sad but glorious episode in Dublin's effort for Irish freedom.

The relatives of the dead man are bearing their cross with great fortitude. His aged mother attended Mass for the repose of his soul at Clarendon street yesterday morning.

Proud Of Her Son

To a Freeman's Journal representative she said: 'I am proud of my son. He died for his country.' [The article continues.]

At the time of Traynor's execution his brother-in-law Patrick O'Sullivan was being held in Canterbury prison. To commemorate Thomas's death he wrote the following poem.

Brother Tom

My heart is full of sorrow, as low I kneel to pray,
For the soul of brother Thomas who God chose to call away,
He had carried his cross for Ireland 'till his time had come to go,
To take his reward in Heaven - God had ordained it so,

May the Blessed Virgin Mary, the Mother of us all,
Protect his wife and children for fear that they should fall,
Intercede for the soul of Thomas and those souls gone on before,
And to our unhappy country send peace for ever more.[7]

The following is an account of visits to Traynor by the Sisters of Charity.

Friends who visited the prisoners in Mountjoy declare that none met death more bravely than Thomas Traynor. He was aged 39 years and left a young wife (about the same age) and ten children. He was an ideal husband and father, devoted to his home and family. His wife is a convert. He left her his rosary beads and asked her to say it every day that Our Lady might make her strong in the Faith. 'I laid no commands on her,' he said, 'but I requested that she should not live with her mother who is still a Protestant, for fear there might be danger to the Children's Faith.' He was confident that all the suggestions made to her by him and his mother would be carried out.

He had studied the character of each of his children and told his friends how he handled each character. He had two violins for the use of himself and his children, also three sets of fretwork for the boys. 'I believe in keeping them usefully employed.' One boy also played the pipes. (On visiting his home after his death, his friends found it just as he had described. The walls were decorated with fretwork and cork frames made by him and the boys. There were also little games for the children made by his own hands.) 'If my home were not happy,' he said, 'I would not stay in it.'

Thomas Traynor with some of his family.
Photo taken circa 1913.

He was only allowed short interviews with his wife. Long conversations with her made him sad. 'I leave my wife and children to God and the Irish Republic. It is a big price to have to pay, but not too big for Heaven.'

His holy old Mother has been a daily communicant for 30 years. She gave him great consolation by telling him that he only did his duty.

Sometimes he looked sad while his friends were talking to him but the mention of Heaven instantly brought a smile to his face.

'Since his death,' writes a special friend, 'I called one day at his workplace. There I found his two oldest sons busily engaged working at their trade. The eldest of the two pointed to his Father's watch hanging on a nail in the wall; the same on which his Father used to keep it. The boys were very sad, but proud of their Father, and determined to do their best for their Mother.' [8]

In response to the application for the body of Thomas Traynor the following letter was issued.

25th April, 1921
re/ Thomas Traynor Deceased

Sir,

With reference to your letter of the 25th April, I am directed by His Excellency to refer you to the Provisions pf section 6 of the Capital Punishment Act, 1868, and to say that it is regretted that your request cannot be complied with.

I am,

Sir
Your obedient Servant
A.C. [Under Secretary Andy Cope]

To: Michael Noyk, Esp., L.L.B.,
Solicitor,
Chambers Star Assurance Buildings,
12 College Green,
Dublin. [9]

In the run up to the execution of Kevin Barry republicans argued that as a prisoner of war Barry should not be executed. As a result of the British policy of executions the IRA began a policy of direct retaliation. A few days after the execution of Patrick Moran on 14 March 1921, there was an ambush at Keadue, Roscommon, in which three policemen were killed.[10] At Clifden, County Galway, two policemen were killed in reprisal for Thomas Whelan's execution. They were Constable Reynolds who was 33 years old, married and from Roscommon, and Constable Sweeney who was 24 and single from Aughrim, County Galway.[11] In April, after Traynor's court martial, a police district inspector, Gilbert Potter, was captured by the IRA and held captive. Potter was 43 years old and married with four children. He had been in the police for 21 years. The IRA had hoped to exchange Potter for Traynor, however, no deal was struck. When Traynor was executed, the IRA, in language strongly reminiscent of that used in statements issued by Dublin Castle, announced the trial and execution of Potter.

Irish Independent, 29 April 1921

REPORTED FATE OF MISSING OFFICER, 'SENTENCED TO DEATH'

'Dist. Inspector Gilbert Potter, having been legally tried and convicted, was sentenced to death, which sentence was duly carried out on Wed., 27th April.'

That was the statement contained in a type-written letter which Mrs. Potter, wife of D.I. Potter, Cahir, received yesterday in a plain envelope unstamped. The note which bore the Cahir postmark, added that during the time of custody the officer was well treated and shown every consideration. The address on the letter was written in Irish, and at the end the notification was signed 'O.C.' Greatly upset by this intimation, Mrs. Potter, who has young children is confined to bed. The district inspector had been stationed in Cahir for a number of years, and was very popular. He did much it is stated to keep the town quiet.

Disappeared In Ambush

Inquiries at Dublin Castle last night, elicited the reply that there was no information on the subject. The Castle weekly review, issued yesterday contained the following reference to the ambush in which Mr. Potter disappeared

'On 22nd inst. a party of 15 military with a G.S. wagon, were ambushed at Curraghclonney, Cahir, by about 100 armed men; but after a short engagement, in which 3 soldiers were wounded (one mortally), the attack was abandoned.

A district inspector of the R.I.C. who was motoring on the road from Clogheen in his private car ran into the ambush, and has not since been heard of. His car, which was found near the scene, bore several bullet marks.'

Mr. Potter was son of the late Rev. Mr. Potter, Letterkenny, Dean of Raphoe.

On 8 May, Potter's widow received a parcel containing her husband's diary, will, signet ring, his gold watch and a letter to her. The remains of Potter were exhumed from a secret grave and then buried in Cahir on 30 August 1921.[12]

DI Potter, executed by the IRA in reprisal for the execution of Thomas Traynor.

THOMAS TRAYNOR

It was early, early, on a Monday morn
As the birds all sang in the flush of dawn
On a Monday morning, on the gallows high
Brave Thomas Traynor was led forth to die.

Led forth to die in his manhood's prime;
No flag did flutter, no bell did chime,
But the Rosary spoken, came sweet and clear
From the people all gathered round the jail gate near.

Let my loving wife neither weep nor sigh,
For Ireland's sake I am proud to die,
I am proud to die though my children dear
A father's voice never more shall hear.

Fight not for vengeance when I am dead,
Nor from duty's path let your minds be led,
But fight for freedom – for the cause I die –
And place your trust in Great God on high.

Like music soft on the morning air
The people's voices rise in murmured prayer,
The bolt is drawn, tight the fatal cord,
Thomas Traynor's soul is now safe with God.

The sacrifice for his land is made,
In the prison grounds is his body laid,
With the sainted martyrs of liberty –
Who died that Ireland might soon be free.[13]

*Photo of Thomas Traynor's widow and their
ten children taken one week after his execution.*

RESCUE OF SEAN HOGAN AT KNOCKLONG RAILWAY STATION, 13 MAY 1919

After the attack at Soloheadbeg on 21 January 1919 that marked the start of the War of Independence, Dan Breen, Sean Treacy, Seamus Robinson and Sean Hogan went 'on the run'. The attack was the first step in a campaign characterised by guerrilla warfare carried out by small groups attacking Crown forces and then disappearing into the countryside or city streets. After nearly four months of evading a huge effort by police and military to capture them the four stopped off at Rossmore, County Tipperary. On the evening of Sunday 11 May they went to a local dance. After their night away Breen, Treacy and Robinson returned to Rossmore. However, Hogan went on to another house in Annefield. After breakfast on Monday morning six police arrived at this well-known nationalist household for a routine raid. Hogan, who was armed, tried to escape but was captured.

Knocklong Railway Station.

Initially the police were unaware of the identity of the man they had in custody, but they soon identified him as one of the Soloheadbeg men. They prepared to bring him by train to Cork for detention and further questioning. He was brought from Thurles to Limerick Junction railway station by Sergeant Wallace and Constables Enright, Ring and Reilly. The party boarded the train for Cork. Meanwhile Hogan's three comrades had committed themselves to a rescue. They had assembled a group of Volunteers from the Galbally district at the quiet railway station of Knocklong to await word of Hogan's transfer. The message they were waiting for did not arrive. However, when a Cork-bound train arrived at 8.13 p.m., a Volunteer on the train signalled to the rescue party that Hogan was on the train.

By the time the train left Sean Hogan had been rescued. However, the rescue was not straightforward. When Sean Treacy, followed by another Volunteer Eamon O'Brien, entered the compartment and told Hogan to come with them, Constable Enright put a gun to the prisoner's head and tried to use him as a shield. Treacy and O'Brien shot Enright. One bullet went through his heart and he died instantly. Sergeant Wallace, who was 44 years old and had more than 25 years service, then struggled with Treacy in the closely confined quarters of the compartment. In this desperate struggle Treacy was shot in the neck. In a decisive effort Treacy turned the gun on Wallace and shot him twice in the stomach. Wallace fell mortally wounded. In a confrontation on the platform, Constable Ring had shot Dan Breen. Constable Reilly was attacked by the other Volunteers, including Edmond Foley, and he collapsed unconcious. In a matter of minutes the confrontation was over.[14] One newspaper reported the incident as follows.

CONSTABLE SHOT DEAD
STARTLING OCCURRENCE AT SOUTHERN RAILWAY STATION
ATTACK ON TRAIN

Prisoner Gets Away

A sensational occurrence is reported from Co. Limerick, involving the death of one Policeman and the wounding of two others. It would appear that a sergeant and three Constables were escorting a prisoner named John Hogan from Thurles to Cork gaol on the 4.50 pm train from Dublin yesterday, when at Knocklong station, the carriage in which they were seated was rushed by a party of armed men, and a fierce encounter took place. In the struggle one constable was shot dead and the sergeant was so seriously wounded that there is little hope of his recovery. He was taken to Kilmallock Union Hospital. The Prisoner, John Hogan, it is alleged, was taken away from the train. Another constable, who was badly injured made an effort at pursuit and fired several shots, with what effect it is not yet known. Great excitement and alarm prevailed among the passengers and those on the station platforms.

When the train reached Cork, an hour after its scheduled time, the carriage in which the occurrence took place was taken in charge by the police authorities. Many bullet-marks and blood splashes bore evidence of a deadly and terrible struggle.[15]

Plaque commemorating the rescue at Knocklong.

After the rescue, police and troops poured into the area. They were despatched in lorries to scour the districts of Knocklong, Galbally, Ballylanders, Emly and the Glen of Aherlow. Sergeant Wallace 'lingered' until Wednesday when he succumbed to his injuries. Wallace was buried in a graveyard near Curraghroe, County Roscommon. The King sent a note of sympathy to the families of the deceased.[16] At Templemore Father Kiely asked for prayers for the two dead policemen and asked what the country was coming to when men discharging their duties lost their lives in such a manner? According to the priest no matter how much people tried to disguise the killings with a political cover the Knocklong killings were 'cold blooded murder and a crime against God and Man'.[17] Dr Harty, the Archbishop of Cashel, denounced the killings 'as crimes against Ireland' and asked the young men of Ireland not to stain the fair name of their native land by deeds of bloodshed.[18] After the rescue Treacy, Breen, Robinson and Hogan went on the run again and later re-emerged to become some of the greatest exponents of guerrilla warfare. In September six men were arrested for the attack. Two were ultimately convicted and executed. They were Edmond Foley, who was an unarmed participant in the attack, and Patrick Maher who had taken no part in it.

Edmond Foley was born in 1895 in Galbally, County Limerick. He was the eldest of William and Margaret Foley's four children. They were a prosperous family who had a farm. In 1918 Edmond was one of the first men in the area to enlist in the Irish Volunteers. A sociable person he often attended dances. Described as fair-haired and good-looking he had a girlfriend, Eileen O'Connell. After the rescue of Hogan, Foley went on the run, ignoring any suggestions that he should leave the country. During this time he was made godfather to one of his cousin's children; the child had to be brought to an isolated field for the christening. In September 1919 he was captured when he went back to the family farm to help his father.

Patrick Maher and Edmond Foley.

At the time of his arrest Patrick Maher was 30 years old. He was born in Glenlara, Knocklong, and attended Glenbrohane National School. Maher had one half-sister and two half-brothers. He was described as 'quiet, gentle and good'. He was a member of the Cush Company of the Irish Volunteers. Maher lived near Knocklong and delivered eggs for a living. At the time of the Knocklong rescue there was a strike on at a local creamery, as part of his work Maher crossed the picket line which made him unpopular with some in the area. Indeed feelings were so high that at one point he was offered police protection. Later, at his court martial, it was an important point made in his defence, 'Of all places in the world if Paddy Maher had wanted to commit murder would he have committed it in the very place where even the blades of grass must have known him, and he also at the very time being a boycotted man in Knocklong? The only friends he had in the place were his employer and the butcher O'Byrne, the only men in Knocklong who would supply him with even a cigarette or any goods. You are asked to believe that a man in the middle of a hostile crowd like that, every one of whom on account of this labour dispute would be content to knife him if he did anything wrong – you are asked to say that this man under those circumstances would have taken part in this murder.' [19] It was reported that in September 1919, Maher had a premonition that there was trouble 'in front of him'. He told his mother this just before he went to bed, within an hour the house was surrounded by Black and Tans and Maher would never see his home again.

City Hall, on left, where nine of the ten men executed were tried. In the background is Dublin Castle.

Foley and Maher were the first of the men who were hanged in Mountjoy to be arrested, however, they were the last ones executed. They were tried in Limerick on two occasions but each time the juries could not agree on a verdict. They were then moved north to Armagh where it was thought there would be a jury more likely to bring in a guilty verdict. However, the trial had to be postponed when one of the key witnesses for the prosecution, Sergeant Reilly, who had been at Knocklong, was kidnapped. They were then moved to Dublin and held in Mountjoy. After the passing of the ROI Act their cases were handed over to the military authorities. (The question of whether cases which had been heard in civil courts could then be handed over to the military had recently been decided in favour of the Crown.) Now, instead of being tried in front of a civilian jury the men would be tried by court martial in front of six British Army officers. Their chances of acquittal had lessened considerably. It is a thought that must have played on their minds in Mountjoy on the mornings when the other eight were executed.

The court martial of Foley and Maher began in City Hall on 15 March. It was the day after the six men had been hanged in Mountjoy and Thomas Traynor had been captured in Brunswick Street. Their court martial lasted five days – the court martial did not sit on Saint Patrick's Day. The case against the two men rested largely on them being identified by three Crown witnesses. Two of these disagreed on what Maher, whom they identified as the leader of the attack, was wearing. It is possible that Maher was mistaken for Dan Breen. Unlike the other eight men executed in Mountjoy, Foley and Maher made lengthy statements to the court.

[Underlining as in the original manuscript]

The Judge Advocate: The accused are entitled to make a statement, and I think we should start with their statements if they wish to make one. Edmond Foley, do you wish to make a statement?

The Accused <u>Foley</u>: Yes. Gentlemen of the Court, I absolutely declare to you that I am innocent of this charge. I want to tell you first of all that I have been 18 months in prison as you are aware, and as the result of my confinement I have been completely broken down in health. I leave it to any medical expert to examine me and he will tell you that I am completely broken down. I am suffering from lumbago in my back and great pains in my inside, and I have been under the doctor's care in the hospital all the time in prison. That is all I have to say about that.

As regards my movements on the 13th May on that evening and that day I want to go into them now in detail. On the day of the shootings I worked in my father's garden all day in company with my brother Willie and the servant boy Corbett. When evening came we finished up work outside as it was raining, and we came into the hagget – that is the hay-barn. I was jobbing round tidying up in the hay-barn. We were all there, my brother, my father, and the working boy, Corbett, and a man came in – it is so long ago now it is very hard to remember everything – <u>a man came in by the name of Denis Daly</u>, a neighbour, and I remember seeing the boy, Corbett, cutting his hair in the hay-barn. In the meantime I was doing various jobs; it being a farm we were beginning to start the summer's work. That would be from say <u>6 o'clock until 7 o'clock, or after 7</u>. <u>I could say I then went into my</u> <u>father's house and had my supper until about 20 minutes after 7, or</u> <u>15 minutes</u> after in the evening.

Mr Lynch: Would that be <u>old time</u>?

The Accused, Foley: Yes, that <u>would be old</u> <u>time</u> [i.e. before daylight savings time was introduced]. I then immediately, as it was customary for me to do, left my house and went as the common saying is over to a neighbour's house. That is what we call it courting. I paid my visit to this neighbour's house where I was often in the habit of going I may tell you after the day's work was over. It was to Mr. Quish's house, which is about 4 or 5 fields away, that is to say about half a mile. I arrived there in <u>or</u>

Edmond Foley.

<u>about 8 o'clock</u>; it may have been before or it may have been a little after. That is <u>old time</u>. I stopped there until about <u>10 o'clock</u>. Mrs Quish was there, her daughter Annie Quish was there, and <u>William</u> <u>Quish was also there</u>. We had various amusements; I think we played cards, and we talked away as usual. I then left that place for my own house at 10 o'clock. <u>I could say I arrived home at half past 10</u>. I went to bed; my brother was in bed; <u>all the family were in bed at the time</u>. I went to bed and slept sound and got up next morning and had my breakfast as usual. I knocked about for a while, but it being a <u>wet day</u> I said 'I will have <u>another run</u> round to <u>Quish's', and I went again there</u> <u>in the morning</u>. In the meantime I had heard about the shooting. We

did not talk about it because I did not know whether it was fact or not. I <u>came back</u> from Quish's. I could not say now exactly what time it would be when I did come back from Quish's, but I remember my father telling me 'The police from Galbally have called here for you, and the military, and they are looking for you.' 'All right', said I. He said 'They want you to report at Galbally; you had better go to the Barracks.' I said certainly I would go to the Barracks, and I then proceeded to the village of Galbally where the Barracks were. I went immediately into the Barracks and I saw the Police Sergeant who has already been examined, Sergeant Kennedy. He asked me my whereabouts last night, and <u>I gave him a complete account of my movements</u>, as I have given it to you now. He says he does not think I did. I really did give him an account, and he said 'That is alright', and he said 'You can go home', and I went away and heard nothing more about it until some time afterwards, I think it would be in the month of June. I was questioned by District Inspector McLean, I think it was. He came to my father's house in a raiding party and they searched the house. I was out working in the garden with the working boy – I do not remember whether my brother was there or not – and two R.I.C. constables came out and said the District Inspector McLean wanted to see me in the house. I went into the house and District Inspector McLean said he wanted me to answer some questions. He asked me first if I would answer them. I said yes I would answer any questions and tell him anything he wanted to know. He questioned me about my various movements on that night, my identity with the volunteer movement – and what else did he ask me?

Mr Best: Did he ask you about the bicycle?

The Accused, Foley: Oh Yes, he questioned me about a bicycle I had. On that day when he came in June, my bicycle was at Crowley's cycle shop at Ballylanders being repaired – because I might mention about that, <u>on the night of the 13th of May when this tragedy took place I had no bicycle</u>. My bicycle was all smashed up and broken up; it was all asunder and the back wheel off, and when the Police

Sergeant Kennedy entered my house on the morning of the 14th of May he could not help seeing it because it was in the back room there without the tyres on or anything else. Now I think I have finished about District Inspector McLean. He went away; but before going he said it was alright, and I heard nothing more about it until I was arrested on the 24th September 1919. The Sergeant told me he charged me with the murder of the Police Constable. I said I had nothing to say. I was taken to Limerick to the Police Barracks there, and we were formally remanded from time to time, and we have been remanded all the time from the 24th September until the 24th October. We thought it very queer during that time being arrested 5 months after the thing happened, and being kept there until the 24th October without any evidence being offered against us.

There is another thing I want to go into now, Sir. It is about our time in Limerick Prison. It is not because I want to attach any blame to the Prison Authorities, or to anyone, but several times when in the prison we asked to be allowed shaving things so as to get a shave, but we never could get them. All the time we were in Mountjoy we were allowed to shave, and after being identified we were allowed to shave. That is the curious part of it, but we were not allowed to shave before being identified. So when we were taken out for identification we had a four weeks growth of beard on us, and anyone would know that we were out of Limerick Prison. We were put in with a crowd of men who seemed to be like Dockers – men working in the Docks – and we were mixed up with them. I had a coat in my hand. I was dressed rather remarkably. I was wearing a heather mixture suit of clothes, long pants, and a brown pair of shoes, a soft hat and a cardigan jacket. We had collars and ties; they had not collars and ties, but ordinary fellows, and here we were with our beards an inch long. We asked several times in Limerick to have our clothes changed, but we were not allowed to, and we had to go in the togs that we had come in, and we had to go without being shaved. Another thing while in the prison at Limerick we noticed that there was a police guard put in there when we came there. Mind you, we used to go out in a yard exercising every day, and <u>several times the police came to the window when we were exercising and were looking out at us</u>, and we objected before we were identified and asked what they were looking out for. One day one of them spoke to Murphy [another of the Knocklong accused, he was acquitted], I think it was. He said 'Good day, Murphy, how are you getting on', or something like that. We objected to the Chief Warder and he said 'I will not have this; this thing will have to be stopped.' So he got a new window put in altogether, and got it glazed. That is all about the prison.

Then we came up for parade. When we were paraded on the 24th October for identification in William Street Barracks, the Police Sergeant, <u>Sergeant Riley</u> [Reilly] – I am really surprised at him – first swore definitely the other day that he was not put <u>into the cell after identification</u>. He failed to identify us; he went up <u>that</u> way first, and then down again, and then he went round to our backs, and he failed to identify any one of us. He swore definitely the other day that he was not put into the cell with us where we were. I swear on oath that he was put in the cell with us, and he was in the cell with us for a <u>quarter of an hour</u> after identification.

There is something else I wanted to say, but it is so hard to think of it all.

The President: Do not hurry; take as much time as you like.

Mr O'Connor: What happened in the yard during identification?

The Judge Advocate: I do not think you should suggest anything to him, Mr O'Connor. He is not being examined, you know.

Mr Lynch: It is extremely difficult for him to remember everything. We have his statement.

The President: We will give him lots of time.

The Accused, Foley: One of the witnesses, Morris, I think, said he did not hesitate to identify me in William Street Barracks in Limerick. He did hesitate to identify me, because he passed down along the crowd of fellows that way, and I think he had this man here (indicating the accused, Maher) picked out, but he passed along and <u>he failed to pick me out. He then went to our backs and he picked me out, and laid his hand on my shoulder. He swore the other day that he did not hesitate to identify me, but I swear that he did hesitate to identify me</u>.

I do not think that there is anything else I have to say, only that here I am today, arrested on the 24th September 1919, and indeed I am sure that all very well know that a prison is not a very nice place to be in. Here I am today in March 1921 physically wrecked in health. That is all I have to say to you.

The Judge Advocate: Maher, do you wish to say anything?

The Accused, Maher: Yes, Sir.

The Judge Advocate: Make any statement you wish to make.

The <u>Accused, Maher</u>: I wish to tell you that I have been for the last 18 months as innocent of this charge against me as a newborn child. That is God's truth. Also I wish to say that I can go in the witness box and swear before God that I have never fired a shot with any firearm in my life. I also have to say <u>I never had a rifle or revolver in my possession</u>, and I think everyone, or everyone who knows me, knows that if a policeman was shot it is God's truth I never shot him. I have worked for Mr Riordan for years, and I remember the day in question. I went to work that morning as usual. It was my business to attend the egg market at the railway station, and to keep a book of all the sales and purchases, and I can bring the books here to prove that I was there all day. <u>I finished my work at half past 6</u>, and I remember on locking the door of the store seeing a man I know there and bidding him good evening. I was wearing a <u>green coat and grey pants and vest and a dark frieze overcoat and cap</u>, and I had a collar and tie on. I then proceeded to my boss, Mr Riordan's house and handed him the keys of the store and my books. He was drinking his tea at the time; he always has his tea between 6 and 7 o'clock. He is head Creamery Manager for Mr Cleeves. There was a strike on at Cleeves at the time, and as I did not join in it, myself and my boss were boycotted at that period. They would not even let me get a drink at Harris's, as I think the Sergeant knows, and do you think, gentlemen, I am going up to the station and all the men around having me boycotted and threatened with my life - would I go to the station to rescue a prisoner. Would anybody believe that? Another thing is I had no connection at all with Hogan the man who was rescued, and knew nothing about him…

When I handed the keys to Mr Riordan I asked him 'May I go to the Limerick Junction Races tomorrow?' He told me I might but I should have to come down early and do a half-day's work first. I then proceeded homewards with W. Riordan that is the boy who was working with me at the egg store – <u>I live with my mother about 5 miles from Knocklong</u>. When we got to the Cross of the Tree I remember meeting John Gainey who was going in the car to meet the train from Cork. I met him <u>about three miles from my home, and I saluted him</u>. We then went into <u>Mulvihill's public house</u> about half-a-mile further on to give an account to Mrs Mulvihill about the price of eggs. Mrs Mulvihill was inside the shop and I had a bottle of Dry Ginger Ale and Mr W. Riordan who was with me had a bottle of stout. Mrs Mulvihill asked me the price of the eggs and I told her, and Tom O'Brien was standing in the shop, and he says 'Did you meet Mulvihill's car' and I said I did. He said the car had gone to meet the Cork train. We remained there a quarter-of-an-hour and then proceeded. I parted with my man Riordan at Pinkers Cross he had to go that way, and about 100 yards from my own house I met a man <u>Michael Ryan</u> standing in his own yard, and he asked me about the strike. I had got 100 yards further to go home. My mother and sister always have my supper ready when I go in, and I had my supper, and I remember my mother saying as I was sitting down 'You had better put the donkey in the car in the morning and take it.' <u>When I had my supper I proceeded to Glenlara Cross</u> half a mile further back to carry a newspaper to a man named James Clifford, a farmer. By the same token he could see me from his own gate coming from my house, and I met him half way between my house and his own house. I gave him the paper and we proceeded a little way along the road towards the Cross, where we <u>met Philip Ryan and Edmond Crawford</u>. We were going to have a game of ball, but the road was not suitable. <u>We were there between a quarter of an hour and a half an hour when the first car arrived from the train with Jim Crawford and Edmond Quinlan... Jim Crawford told me about the shooting and about the prisoner being rescued, and Edmond Quinlan also told me</u>. Soon after that I left them and went up to Mr Burns to give him an account of the price of eggs. I often buy stuff off him. I proceeded up there and stayed there until it was time for me to go home. When I got home my people were in bed. I went to bed and got up in the morning and got my donkey and car and <u>started off for Knocklong</u>. On the way I met Michael Ryan the man I was talking to the night before and he also informed me about the shooting. I proceeded with the donkey and car and went and met W. Riordan at 7 o'clock at Pinker's Cross as we had arranged to do the night before and told him he might be able to come to the Races with me. I went to my boss and got the keys of the store and my books, and my boss said '<u>You were a lucky man to be away last night on account of the shooting here.</u>' I proceeded to the store and opened the store, and Mr Burns came in, the man I was speaking to the night before, and he says to me 'By God you are a lucky man to have gone home last night because if you had been here you might have been shot.' So I worked hard that morning and took some eggs to the station. I would not go into the Creamery that morning to bring out the horse to take the eggs to the station owing to the police and soldiers being there and the picket. After finishing my work I went to the races at the Junction and I had a good day. I backed four winners. On my way home that day I went to Mulvihill's public house and we were talking about my being there the night before and being there before Conn arrived. After that, I worked every day until some time in June when I had to stop work for a couple of days because the crowd got too angry with me, and the boss said he would get police protection for me if I worked and I said I would. The next day the boys found out that I was going to get police protection and when I opened the door the next morning there was a notice that if I worked under police protection I should be shot that night. I told my boss I would not work under police protection, but would take the eggs at the risk of my life, and I worked at the store every day until some time in June when a man named Shanahan was arrested on this charge that we are here for, and he was taken to Cork prison. In June Inspector McLean and the Sergeant came to my house and the Inspector said 'I should like to search your house', and he asked me my movements and I told him and about Mrs Mulvihill's and the other people being there, and he asked me what time I arrived home and I told him. This overcoat that I have here was hanging up on a nail and the Sergeant took it down and asked me if it was my coat. <u>I said it was, and he then drew attention to this hole here, and made out that it was a bullet hole, but it is only a tear made by a nail, that is all</u>. I gave my statement to Inspector McLean and heard nothing more – I worked every day after that at the store – until the <u>24th September</u>, when Sergeant Queenan called for me and arrested me and took me to Limerick. <u>I agree with all that Mr Foley has said about our treatment by police and the military</u>. They made us very comfortable as they could, and treated us very decently, and we have never been insulted by police, soldier, or warder. That is 18 months ago. I think we were a month in the prison after we were arrested, and <u>during that month we never had a shave</u> and we were wearing our beards, and we were exercised in a small yard about 35 feet by 20, and there was not another prisoner amongst us except one, a prisoner named Joseph Maddon, another murder charge, and Mr Lynch defended him afterwards. There were five of us altogether and we were exercising in that yard, and there were three windows looking into that yard, and sometimes we were taken out for identification. <u>I saw two police looking out of the window on this side one day</u>. We drew the attention of the warder to it and the warder said 'I will stop that', and the day after there was a new window put in and it was whitewashed so that none could look out, but the whitewash was rubbed off again and they were peeping out the same as before. We were about a month in prison when we were taken for identification to William Street Barracks. I very nearly had an accident with the motor car in going and I got a great fright and was very pale when I got there. We were put in the lock up, and the surprising part of it was that when we were first taken to William Street Barracks we were not lined up but for a quarter of an hour we were put in a cell, <u>and 4 or 5 people came to the door and were peeping in</u>. Then we were taken out into the yard and lined up and <u>I was put first in the rank, although they told me I could line up wherever I liked</u>. They came out to identify us and there were two or three police at the door as they came out, and <u>they made me take off my top-coat</u> before my identification and put it on the form – after the identification we were sitting down on the form – <u>so that I had no top-coat for identification</u>. I asked a man who was standing alongside me during identification 'What is all this about?' and he said 'Identification, and they are after picking me out'. <u>I was very sorry to hear Sergeant Reilly swearing that he was not in the cell with us after identification, because he is a straight man, and I would not like to say anything against him, but he was put into the cell with us himself and another constable, and they stayed in for a quarter of an hour.</u> We were sent back to the prison again, and brought up for second identification in the morning very early, and we were lined up in William Street Barracks along with about 13 men, and a soldier chap came up I suppose for identification again, and he walked up and down several times and picked out no one. We were put back into the cell again and then we were sent back to the prison and left in prison for 3 months before we were returned for trial. Then we were sent to Belfast and from Belfast to Armagh, and Armagh to here, and here we are today after 18 months. That is all I have to say to you, gentlemen.[20]

In early April the father of Sergeant Wallace who had been killed at Knocklong wrote to General Macready, Commander of Forces in Ireland, about Foley and Maher.

> *Curraghroe*
> *Strokestown*
> *Co Roscommon*
>
> *Hon. Sir,*
>
> *The late Sergeant Wallace killed at Knocklong was my Son. No father ever reared a better boy or one kinder to his father. I am now over eighty years of age. My daughter and another boy live with me. We were overpowered with grief when we first heard of the Sergeant's death. The tragedy will press heavier on me during the remaining years of my life; if any lives are sacrificed on account of my Son's death.*
>
> *My Son and daughter join with me in imploring you to be Clemant and merciful to those who have been tried in connection with the tragedy. May God forgive those who were really guilty. I do. I am Hon. Sir*
>
> *Your respectful Servant*
> X [for signature]
>
> *Edward Wallace*
> *Witness to mark Kate Wallace daughter of Edward Wallace* [21]

When the men were informed of their death sentences they were permitted their first visitors since their arrests nearly two years before.

Foley, whose health had deteriorated while in prison, wrote to his sister from Mountjoy.[22]

[no date]

H.M. Prison,
Mountjoy,
Thursday.

My dearest Ellie,

I suppose you know by this time that we are sentenced to death, although our innocence was proved beyond all doubt. Well, don't shed one tear for me, only pray for me. I hope you are all as happy as what we are. Oh! we are quite happy.

It doesn't matter much what they do to me because my life is a one of suffering. I am in a terrible state with my back but I get ease sometimes. Father and mother are looking fine really. I wouldn't know Willie he got to be such a big boy. Tell Timmie and all the friends I will write to them soon. Give them all my very best wishes. You can write and send parcels as usual. Send some tobacco and matches.

Very best love to father, mother, Sara, Willie and self.
Your loving brother,

Ned.

H.M.Prison,
Mountjoy,
31st May, '21.

My dearest father and mother,

I expect you have already seen by the day's paper that our sentence has been confirmed. We are now in the condemned cell but we haven't been yet told when we are to be executed.

We are ever so happy, T.G. [Thank God], quite content and fully resigned to God's holy will. Our guard and everyone are ever so kind to us. I just had Ellie's letter now. We get our food from the prison hospital. My health has improved – the lumbago was almost leaving me.

I expect you will call to see us. Now don't anyone worry a bit about me. I am going to my dearest home, heaven. It's but a matter of a few years until we all meet there. Give my very best wishes to all friends and neighbours. Fondest love to my own dear father and mother, Sara, Ellie and Willie. Farewell.

I remain, ever loving son,
Ned.

P.S. Will write again tomorrow.

Foley and Maher were to be executed on the same morning as William Mitchell. Mitchell was a Black and Tan who had been convicted of killing a Justice of the Peace in Dunlavin Co. Wicklow while trying to extort money from him (an accomplice committed suicide the day after the killing). Despite the large numbers of civilians killed by the police and military during the War of Independence, Mitchell was the only member of the Crown forces found guilty of murder and executed during the entire period. Mitchell had the dubious distinction of being the last person executed by the British in Ireland before the Treaty.

Irish Independent, 7 June 1921

THREE EXECUTIONS IN DUBLIN TODAY
KNOCKLONG MEN'S COURAGE
THEIR FAREWELL

Interviews with their Relatives

Scenes near the Jail

Unless there is an 'eleventh hour' reprieve Edmond Foley and Patrick Maher as well as Const. W. Mitchell will be hanged in Mountjoy Prison this morning.

A petition for a reprieve of Messrs. Foley and Maher has been signed by upwards of 2000 persons composed of influential sections in Co. Limerick.

Both prisoners in bidding farewell to their relatives yesterday showed wonderful cheerfulness courage, and while again declaring their innocence, expressed pleasure at giving their lives for Ireland.

Scenes Near Prison

Crown Forces Active

The hour of execution of Messrs. Foley and Maher has been fixed for 7 a.m. and of Const. Mitchell at 8 a.m.. Very Rev. J. Canon Waters, Prison Chaplain, has arranged for the celebration of Mass for Messrs. Foley and Maher before 6.30 a.m.

Yesterday evening crowds assembled outside the prison gate and recited the Rosary. Armed sentries appeared on the road of the prison shortly before 9 p.m. and a detachment of troops on foot held up and searched men in the vicinity of the prison. All, with the exception of a few women saying prayers for the Knocklong prisoners, were obliged to go outside the outer gate.

Troops Disperse Crowd

Later a huge crowd assembled, but, they were quickly moved by the troops. Mrs. Maher, accompanied by some lady friends, was the last to leave the prison. She showed remarkable fortitude, and sympathetic spectators made inquiries regarding the two men.

It is stated that the executioners, Roberts and Ellis arrived in the prison on Sunday.

Mr. Power solr., Kilmallock, who is acting for the Knocklong prisoners states that over 2,000 signatures have now been received to the memorial for their reprieve.

They include the clergy of all denominations, many professional gentleman, landed gentry, and ex-army officers, and J.P.'s who hold their commissions, all resident in the Co. Limerick, as well as the D.J., of the county, Mr. John Ryan, of Scarteen, Master of the Stag Hounds.

FAREWELL MESSAGE

Visits of Relatives

The last message jointly signed by Messrs. Foley and Maher, 'to all the boys' reads –

'Fight on, struggle on, for the honour, glory, and freedom of dear old Ireland. Our hearts go out to all our dear old friends. Our souls go to God at 7 o'c. in the morning, and our bodies when Ireland is free shall go to Galbally. Our blood shall not be shed in vain for Ireland, and we have a strong presentiment going to our God that Ireland will soon be free and we gladly give our lives that a smile may lighten the face of our dear 'Dark Rosaleen.' Farewell, Farewell, Farewell.'

Prisoners And Relatives

The father of Foley, an active man of 62 years, when seen last night after his final interview with his son, showed no sign of distress, and expressed himself 'pleased that his innocent boy should give his life for the freedom of his country.' His son, he said, was thoroughly reconciled to his fate. Mr Foley was accompanied on the occasion of his visit to the prison by his wife and two daughters, Sarah and Ellen, and his son William.

When they entered the sitting room where the condemned man was in charge of a warder their son affectionately embraced each of them, and was in a cheery mood, never exhibiting the least depression or fear. He actually said he did not desire a reprieve, for he believed he was going straight to heaven. He expressed strong hopes of the future happiness of his country.

Though his innocence was well known, he forgave everyone who gave evidence against him and spoke in high terms of the treatment he had received from the prison staff and the Auxiliary police, and he also expressed appreciation of the able manner in which his defence had been conducted by Messrs. Lynch, K.C , Best, K.C. Power, B.L., and J. O'Connor, B.L.

Request to Brother

Mr. Foley said that his boy met his mother as if he were going to a festival, and requested that his brother should take up his cross and follow him firm and fearless to the last.

'I am proud of the son I reared,' said Mr. Foley who added that he was going to suffer in the same spirit as such gallant men as Kevin Barry, Moran, Whelan, Thomas Traynor, and others. When his son was dead his rosary beads would be handed over to him. His son had asked him to wear them during his lifetime. His son gave him devotional objects and had asked him to secure a plot in the burial ground at Galbally.

P. Maher's Courage

Mrs. Maher, her daughter, and Thomas Quinlan, stepbrother, visited Patrick Maher yesterday. He, like Foley, was happy and cheerful, and affectionately embraced his relatives. He did not seem much concerned with his fast approaching doom, and gave them clearly to understand that it was a pleasure to him to make the supreme sacrifice and offer up his innocent life for Ireland's Freedom. He could die for no better object and in the next world he would pray for the success of the cause.

Dignified Protest

He wished to thank the prison staff and the Auxiliaries for their kind treatment of him.

He considered it unfair that he should be kept in prison for 21 months, tried twice and a third time by court martial in face of the fact that himself and Foley were two innocent men.

The parting between the aged mother and Maher was a pathetic one but the man never wavered, remaining self-possessed and smiling until the relatives left the apartment.

The night before the executions the hotels in which the Foley and Maher families were staying were raided. The men in each family were arrested, apparently as a precaution against a rescue bid.

From 5.30 a.m. on the morning of the executions people began to gather outside the prison in what had become an almost ritualistic routine. A little after 6 a.m. Edmond Foley's parents and his two sisters arrived at the prison gates. Mrs Maher and her daughter arrived soon after. Hymns were sung in the by now brilliant sunlight. British soldiers guarded the roof of the prison. At 7 a.m. the executioners entered the cell and led the two men to the execution chamber. When the executioners entered the cell, Maher reportedly said in a clear voice, 'I am innocent.' Foley said, 'God save Ireland and grant her freedom soon.' The two stepped under the ropes on the platform and their heads were covered with hoods and the lever was pulled which opened the trapdoor. Father MacMahon anointed the bodies. He removed a pair of scapulars from Foley. It had been given by one of the Auxiliary guards to Foley and was returned to him. At 8 a.m. William Mitchell was hanged. It was reported that he faced his death bravely. He left behind a wife and child. At 8.15 a warder tried to pin the official notice of the execution on the prison door but it was snatched from his hands.

Plaque outside Mountjoy's hanghouse.

In later years, Dan Breen, one of the leaders of the Knocklong rescue wrote,

> 'Paddy Maher went to the scaffold with [Foley] for the same 'crime' even though he had not hand, act or part in the rescue of Sean Hogan. Both gladly gave their lives for Ireland and their brave words spoken from the gallows will keep their memory green in the hearts of Irish patriots. May they rest in peace.'[23]

Notes to the text

1. Public Record Office (PRO), Colonial Office (CO) 904/43.

2. Sean O'Mahony, *Frongoch: University of Revolution*, FDR Teoranta, Dublin, 1987, p. 49.

3. Kilmainham Gaol and Museum.

4. PRO, War Office (WO) 71/366.

5. *Freeman's Journal*, 25 April 1921.

6. Ibid.

7. Courtesy of Traynor Family.

8. National Library of Ireland (NLI), MS Accession number 5140.

9. General Prison Board (GPB) 1921, 3345.

10 Michael O'Callaghan, *For Ireland and Freedom, Roscommon's Contribution to the Fight for Independence*, Colm O'Callaghan, Boyle, pp. 86-88.

11. Richard Abbott, *Police Casualties in Ireland 1919-1922*, Mercier Press, Cork, 2000, p. 209.

12. Ibid. pp. 225-226.

13. *Waterfront News*, April 1966. In the wake of the State funerals the Traynor family intend to add two verses to this ballad to bring it up to date.

14. For details of the escape see Desmond Ryan, *Sean Treacy and the 3rd Tipperary Brigade*, The Kerryman, Tralee, 1945, pp. 90-107.

15. *Freeman's Journal*, 14 May 1919.

16. Ibid.

17. *Irish Independent*, 19 May 1919.

18. *Freeman's Journal*, 16 May 1919.

19. PRO, WO 71/365.

20. Ibid.

21. PRO, CO 904/41.

22. Both of Ned Foley's letters courtesy of the Foley family.

23. Dan Breen, *My Fight for Irish Freedom*, Anvil, Dublin, 1989, p. 59.

Conclusion

For 80 years members of the families of the ten men executed in Mountjoy could only visit the resting place of their loved one with prior permission from the Mountjoy Prison authorities. On 14 October 2001, the ten were disinterred, one was reburied in Ballylanders and nine in Glasnevin cemetery, the place of rest of many leading figures in Irish history. For the first time the graves of the ten are readily accessible to the families and to anyone else who wants to pay their respects. The story of how this came about concludes the story of the ten men hanged for Ireland in Mountjoy Prison during 1920–21.

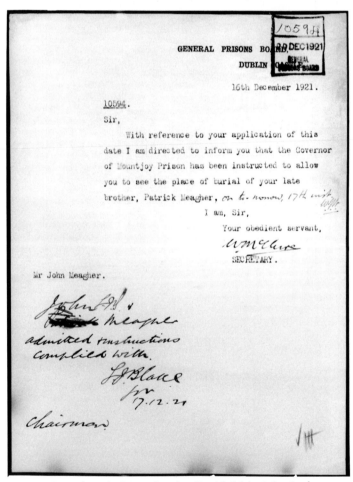

Letter from the Prison Board to Patrick Maher's brother.[1]

Immediately after the ten executions in Mountjoy, the families, or their representatives, handed in letters asking for the remains of their brothers, fathers, husbands and sons for reburial outside the prison. At the time each was informed that under Clause 6 of the Capital Punishment Act the body of the executed person must be buried in the grounds of the prison and therefore their request could not be complied with. After the signing and ratification of the Treaty, power was handed over by the British to the new Provisional Government. In the hope that the new Government would want to see the remains of their comrades given a fitting resting place, some families made immediate applications.

Within a fortnight of taking over Dublin Castle, Michael Collins received the following letter from Emmet Dalton a prominent figure in the War of Independence and the new Provisional Army.

Óglaigh na hÉireann
27-1-22
M. Collins

I have a letter from a Mrs. Quinlan mother of the late Patrick Maher (who was executed in Mountjoy with Foley) requesting that the remains be removed and that she be facilitated towards this end.

In all probability I may expect others. Can you give me any advice or instructions?

J.E. Dalton.
Chief Liaison Officer.

[Handwritten note at end of letter]
sent phone message in reply as follows:
re. Above, the whole matter of the remains of the men executed will be taken up at the same time and a public announcement made. Of course it will be a very big task.[2]

In response to an application by the Wolfe Tone Memorial Committee, Collins gave his support for the 'disinterment of the bodies of all the men shot in Easter Week and executed since'.[3]

(s 4199)   *OIFIG AN UACHTARIAN.*

21ˢᵗ February 1922.

To:

MINISTER FOR DEFENCE.

A Chara,

     <u>*RE-INTERMENT OF EXECUTED MEN.*</u>

I am directed by Mr. Collins to acknowledge receipt of your letter of the 20ᵗʰ inst. (A.1323) in above matter.

Several days ago Mr. Collins wrote to the Wolfe Tone Memorial Committee. We can, of course recover all these bodies. Personally, Mr. Collins would not like the idea of any man being buried inside Jail or Barrack walls.

Do Chara,

SCRIOBHAI. [4]

In a memorandum from the Dáil Cabinet of 24 February 1922, it was decided that all bodies of men buried inside prison walls would be removed when a national ceremony could be arranged for the occasion. However, the issue of the reburials was deferred with the outbreak of the Civil War.

The Ireland that emerged at the end of the Civil War was one radically different from the War of Independence period. The Free State was deeply divided by the bitter conflict. The symbols of the independence movement were now potentially divisive. Both sides could have claimed the remains of the ten in Mountjoy. This may explain why the ten remained in prison graves while four men executed by the Free State during the Civil War, who clearly 'belonged' to one side, were removed from Mountjoy. In 1925 a Government report was prepared on the probable condition of the prison graves of all those executed by the British. According to the report the ten buried in Mountjoy had all been placed in 'porous deal coffins not strongly built and interred in heavy wet clay'. Informed by this report the Executive Council of the Government decided not to exhume the remains.

29ᵗʰ June, 1925.

S.4199 (from Anglo-Irish war)

To

  The Secretary,

    Department of Justice.

A Chara,

With reference to your minute of the 28ᵗʰ instant (ref.261/21) I have to inform you that the following is an extract from the minutes of a meeting of the Executive Council held on the 13ᵗʰ inst. At which the Extern Ministers also were present:

Exhumation of Bodies of persons executed by the British

The opinion of all present at the meeting having been elicited on this matter, it was found that there was general acceptance of the view that the exhumation of the bodies would be impracticable, and a decision was made accordingly.

As it was understood that the Minister for Justice has noted this decision, it was not considered necessary to give you formal intimation thereof.

Mise, le meas,

(Sgd) Diarmuid O hEigceartuigh.

Runai [5]

185

The memorial in Mountjoy with the NGA headstone.

In November 1934, the National Graves Association (NGA) began a long-standing involvement with the ten when they erected a headstone for them. The names of the ten were listed according to their rank. A republican body, the NGA was formed in 1926 'to restore the Graves and Memorials of our Patriot Dead of every generation, to commemorate those who died in the cause of Irish Freedom and to compile a record of such Graves and Memorials'.[6] The NGA has been responsible for over 500 memorials in the 32 counties of Ireland. In addition to a number of the families, the NGA has regularly requested that the remains of the ten be reburied outside of Mountjoy. Requests also came from other sources. In 1951 Dan Breen TD, who had taken part in the rescue at Knocklong in 1919, wrote on behalf of a constituent for the disinterment of Edmond Foley. In its response the Government stated that the graves were well looked after and that it would be impossible to identify the remains. In 1957 students from UCD began an annual commemoration march to Mountjoy. A small group of students was admitted to lay a wreath for former UCD students Kevin Barry and Frank Flood.[7]

In 1960, Sean Kavanagh, the Governor of Mountjoy Prison, wrote to the Minister for Justice, Oscar Traynor. Both men were veterans of the War of Independence. Kavanagh had been in Kilmainham and Mountjoy with the six men executed on 14 March 1921, and Traynor was the brigadier in whose command most of the ten men had served. In the letter Kavanagh requested permission on behalf of some of the prison staff to erect a memorial fitting 'to the memory of Kevin Barry and the nine other members of Óglaigh na hÉireann'. Charles Haughey, on behalf of the Minister for Justice, refused to grant permission. However, in the following year the Government, perhaps prompted by the staff request, decided that it would erect a memorial.

OIFIG AN AIRE DLÍ AGUS CIRT
(Office of the Minister for Justice)
BAILE ÁTHA CLIATH
(Dublin)

          In Mountjoy Prison on Sunday, 8th October, at 11.30 a.m. the President will unveil a Memorial Cross erected in memory of the ten members of Oglaigh na hEireann buried in the prison who gave their lives in the War of Independence.

          The Minister for Justice
               invites

_____

to be present at the ceremony. This invitation may be presented at Mountjoy Prison not later than 11.10 a.m.

6th October, 1961.

Invitation to the unveiling of the new memorial.[8]

On 8 October 1961, a ceremonial unveiling of a new monument took place. The monument was a twelve feet high granite cross and four slabs of Ballinasloe limestone, each slab commemorated one of the four days of executions that took place in Mountjoy. That morning President de Valera was received at the prison gates by the Army Chief of Staff, Major-General Sean Collins-Powell. He was then met at the burial plot by the Taoiseach, Sean Lemass, and the Minister for Justice, Oscar Traynor. Also in attendance were Frank Aiken, Minister for External Affairs, Charles Haughey, Parliamentary Secretary to Minister for Justice, Councillor Robert Briscoe, Lord Mayor of Dublin, former president Sean T O'Ceallaigh and Sean Kavanagh, Governor of the Prison. The 'Presidential Salute' was sounded by the Army Number One Band and de Valera inspected the guard of honour.

Before the cross was unveiled de Valera gave the following speech.

> This is scared ground. Here the bodies of ten young soldiers of the Army of the Republic who, 40 years ago, gave their lives and all that those lives promised, in order that the nation might survive and be free. The older ones amongst us here remember the universal anguish when these young lives were taken, but the pride, too, that the ruthlessness of the enemy was unable to break the spirit of our people.
>
> This, the Easter Week plot at Arbour Hill, the Republican plots in the cemeteries at Glasnevin, Cork, and many other places throughout the country, remind us of the price paid for freedom. May that freedom be forever cherished, and the nation for which the sacrifices were made endure to the end of time. We are grateful to the Minister for Justice, Mr Oscar Traynor, who was the brigadier in whose command most of these young men served, for having seen to it that these graves do not remain unmarked, and for having this cross erected.

Concluding (in Irish) he said:

> May the names of those whose bodies are buried here be always fresh in our memories, and may their souls, together with the souls of all who gave their lives for Ireland, be forever happy with Him, the

symbol of Whose sacrifice stands above their graves. In the name of the Irish people and on their behalf, in mindful reverence, I now unveil this cross.[9]

President de Valera unveiling the Memorial Cross in Mountjoy in October 1961.

The cross was then blessed and the 'Last Post' sounded. The national flag was raised from half mast; Army trumpeters sounded the reveille.

Following the reinterment of Sir Roger Casement in 1966, the question of why the ten remained in Mountjoy was again raised. One member of the public wrote to the Government saying that Kevin Barry should be removed from the grounds of the prison as, 'It is not possible at present to show fitting respect and honour to him when he is resting in an occupied Gaol... I do not think they should lie where British Authority put them, but that they should be removed to a more holier spot in respect.' Another letter stated that 'surely if the British Government can return to Eire the remains of the man they regarded as a traitor, the Government of the Republic can honour Kevin Barry by transferring his remains to Glasnevin Cemetery, and by removing what seems to be an unfounded ban on well-meaning visitors, not sightseers, visiting his grave.' However, the Government continued to reply that they would not disinter the remains and that they were well catered for and now suitably honoured in Mountjoy.[10]

Throughout this period the NGA continued to call on the Government to resolve the issue. However, their efforts gained new impetus when Martessa 'Tess' Kearney became the Secretary of the Association in 1987. Calling the ten in Mountjoy the 'Forgotten Ten' she revived the NGA's campaign to have them disinterred (the name was not strictly true as Kevin Barry was well remembered by the country as a whole and the families of course had not forgotten those who were hanged for Ireland). In 1994, the NGA, with the support of nine of the ten families, submitted exhumation applications to the Minister for the Environment, Michael Smith, who referred the application to the Minister for Justice, Máire Geoghegan Quinn. The Minister replied that she would be happy to comply with the requests provided all the families agreed. At this stage the Moran family decided that they did not want Patrick Moran's remains disturbed. However, in 1998 the family intimated that they would be prepared to reach an accomodation with the other families. After discussions, John O'Donoghue, Minister for Justice, made an announcement outside the hanghouse in Mountjoy Prison on 1 November 2000 (the eightieth anniversary of the execution of Kevin Barry) that with the agreement of each family the ten would be disinterred and reburied with full and appropriate honours in Glasnevin cemetery.

On 28 June 2001, John Fitzgerald, Dublin City Manager (coincidentally a descendent of Edmond Foley), in the presence of representatives of the ten families, gave Sean Aylward, Director of the Irish Prison Service, the official licence to exhume the ten bodies. This ceremony took place in City Hall where nine of the ten men had been tried before military court martials. In August excavations began. Two overriding questions occupied the minds of those involved. Was a map that they had from 1923 indicating the location of the ten graves accurate? If it was indeed accurate what, if anything, would remain of the ten after eighty years of decomposition? Within a couple of weeks they had answers to both. Ten virtually complete skeletons were found where the map had indicated that the ten were buried.

Family representatives outside City Hall with city officials, June 2001.

On Sunday 14 October 2001 at 12.30 p.m., under grey skies and persistent rain, the ceremony that the families of the ten men had waited over 80 years for began in Mountjoy Prison. A short religious service was held at the place where the ten had been buried.

Among those in attendance were the Minister for Justice, John O'Donoghue and the Director of the Irish Prisons Service, Sean Aylward. Against the backdrop of ten coffins draped in the tricolour, Mountjoy's Governor Lonergan began the ceremony by acknowledging that it was right that the bodies should at last be allowed to leave the prison.

Guard of honour in Mountjoy prison.

Six members of each family acted as pall-bearers and brought the coffins, one by one, to the waiting hearses. The gathered families included grandsons, granddaughters, nephews, nieces and grandnephews of the dead men. Many had returned from abroad for the funeral. As the cortège passed through the gates of Mountjoy the prison bell tolled. The prison staff saluted as part of Mountjoy's history came to an end.

Members of Kevin Barry's family carry his coffin to the hearse, Mountjoy.

The cortège proceeded through the streets of Dublin. Many people lined the route and applauded as it passed. At Westmoreland Street around 600 family members followed behind the hearses, which were led by a military band. A guard of honour lined O'Connell Street and flags were flown at half mast. Outside the General Post Office the cortège paused while a cadet guard of honour presented arms and a lone piper played a lament. The cortège then proceeded to the Pro-Cathedral.

Cortège leaving Mountjoy.

Cortège on O'Connell Street, Dublin.

A solemn Requiem Mass was celebrated by Cardinal Cahal Daly. Among the dignitaries present were President Mary McAleese, the Taoiseach Bertie Ahern, Government Ministers and members of the Opposition. The ten coffins were placed in a row before the altar. In his homily Cardinal Daly reflected on the importance of the day.

Coffins with guard of honour outside the Pro-Cathedral, Dublin.

The names of the 10 whom we reinter today are famed in ballad, in song and in story: Kevin Barry of Dublin and Carlow, Thomas Whelan of Clifden, Patrick Moran of Crossna, County Roscommon, Patrick Doyle of Dublin, Bernard Ryan of Dublin, Frank Flood of Dublin, Thomas Bryan of Dublin, Thomas Traynor of Tullow, County Carlow, Edmond Foley and Patrick Maher, both of Galbally, Co. Limerick.

Kevin Barry, 'just a lad of 18 summers', and nine other young men in their 20's and 30's, are today, eighty years after their execution, being given the full honours of a State Funeral. Above all, they are today receiving the overdue dignity of a Christian burial. In this Mass, we commend their souls to God and we commit their bodily remains to consecrated earth, in which they will await the Resurrection. We commend to God also the souls of those who died on the British side.

We think today of the fathers of the Volunteers; we think of their mothers who, as Padraig Pearse said, suffered 'in their coming and in their going'. We think of their families, their relatives, neighbours and neighbourhoods. It is a proud day for all of them. These men died in the belief that their deaths would help to bring into being an Ireland of freedom, of justice, an island in which people would never again feel a need to resort to violent means in order to secure human rights and equal opportunities for all its citizens.[11]

Following the Mass the coffins were placed in the hearses for their final journey to Glasnevin Cemetery. As the cortège passed the Garden of Remembrance it paused and a minute's silence was observed. At the request of his family, Patrick Maher's remains were brought as far as Glasnevin and then to Ballylanders, Co. Limerick, for burial with State honours. At Glasnevin the men's coffins were lowered into the ground one by one in the order in which they had been executed. Before the Taoiseach's oration, wreaths were laid by the families.

Members of the families laying wreaths on grave, Glasnevin.

The burial plot is beside a memorial to Sir Roger Casement and in the shadow of the Daniel O'Connell tower. The graves of the nine are marked by a memorial designed by artist Robert Ballagh. Three volleys of shots were fired over the grave before the Taoiseach began.

> A mhuintir na hÉireann agus a cháirde timpeall an domhain. Táimid bailithe anseo inniu in ómos don deichniúr Óglach a fuair bás ar an gcroch i bPríosún Mhoinseó ar son na saoirse agus ar son na hÉireann. Táimid uilig i láthair chun a dtaisí daonna a chur i gcré sa deireadh le honóir agus le dínit.
>
> Tuigimid go léir cé chomh mór is atáimid faoi chomaoin ag an deichniúr fear óg seo chomh maith le hÓglaigh uile na hÉireann an ama sin, idir fhir agus mhná. Níl an íobairt a rinne siad á ligeant i ndearmad ag muintir na hÉireann agus ní ligfear go deo. An cogadh a throid siad, bhí cúltaca amháin acu nárbh fhéidir neamhshuim a dhéanamh de.

B'shin Ollthoghchán 1918. Bhí a fhios acu go raibh na daoine leo. De thoradh an olltoghcháin sin tháinig ann don Chéad Dáil. Ar Faisnéis Neamhspleáchais na hÉireann a aontú acu dúirt an Ceann Comhairle leis na Teachtaí uilig gur thuig chuile dhuine acu go dtiocfadh cogadh ann de thoradh na Faisnéise.

Thuigeadar san. Bhí siad sásta an cath a chur chun saoirse na tíre a bhaint amach. Bhí sé ráite ag na cumhachtaí móra gur ar mhaithe leis na náisiúin bheaga an Chéad Coghadh Domhanda.

Bhí muintir na hÉireann daingean de go gcaithfí prionsabal an fhéinchinnidh náisiúnta a leathnú chomh fada le hÉirinn. Cuireadh chun báis na fir óga seo le linn Chogadh na Saoirse. Bhí an tír go mór faoi bhrú ag an am agus bhí chuile dhuine aontaithe. Tofa ag muintir na hÉireann, bhí Dáil Éireann ag forbairt léi d'ainneoin cogadh a bheith ar siúl. Bhí an daonlathas á thabhairt i réim sa tír. Bhí solas na saoirse feicthe ag an deichniúir óg seo sula bhfuair siad bás. Thuig siad go mbeadh Éire arís saor agus neamhspleách.

Ní iontas ar bith é mar sin gur mór ag muintir na hÉireann go bhfuil an lá seo tagtha. D'ainneoin go bhfuil deacrachtaí de chuid ár dtréimhse féin againn níl duine féireáilte sa tír seo nach gceapann gur maith an rud é go bhfuilimid ag cur na bhfear seo anseo inniu agus gur mithid é a dhéanamh.

People of Ireland and friends around the world. We are gathered here today in honour of the ten Volunteers who died on the scaffold in Mountjoy Prison in the cause of freedom and the cause of Ireland. We are all here to lay their remains to rest in this soil at last with dignity and honour.

We all understand how much we owe these 10 young men and all the Volunteers of that period, both men and women. Their sacrifice is not being forgotten by the people of Ireland, and it never will.In the war they fought, they had one support that could not be ignored.

That was the mandate for independence from the General Election of 1918. They knew the people were with them. Dáil Éireann was formed from those who were elected, and who were willing or able to attend. When the Declaration of Independence was passed, the Ceann Comhairle of that First Dáil said to the Deputies present that they all understood that war would be the consequence of the Declaration.

The Taoiseach, Bertie Ahern, giving the graveside oration.

They understood that. They were satisfied, if necessary, to fight to liberate the country. The big powers had said that it was for the small nations that the First World War was fought.

The people of Ireland were determined that the principle of national self-determination must also be extended to the Irish nation. During that first session, the Democratic Programme, addressing the economic and social needs of Ireland, was also adopted, at the request of the Labour Movement, 'with a view to a general and lasting improvement in the conditions under which the working classes live and labour'. These 10 young men were executed during the War of Independence. The country was under tremendous pressure at the time. There was a united effort. Meanwhile, elected by the people, Dáil Éireann was developing, in spite of a war going on. Democracy was being put to work. Independent civic institutions, including the Dáil courts, were beginning to function. Before their deaths, the ten had seen the light of freedom. They understood that Ireland would be free and independent.

The 10 men were Kevin Barry, a UCD medical student of 18, with roots in County Carlow; Thomas Whelan from Clifden; Patrick Moran from Roscommon; Patrick Doyle, Bernard Ryan, Frank Flood and Thomas Bryan all from Dublin; Thomas Traynor of Tullow; and Edmond Foley and Patrick Maher, from Galbally, Co Limerick.

It is no wonder to the people of Ireland then that this day has come. Although we have difficulties of our own time, there is no fair person in this country but thinks that it is good that we bury these men with State honours here today, and indeed that it is time we did so.

The Irish State today is discharging a debt of honour that stretches back 80 years. Here in Glasnevin stand the memorials to Irish patriots of the past two centuries, statesmen, soldiers, all those who contributed in many different ways to the onward march of a nation. Nine of the 10 Irish volunteers executed in Mountjoy in 1920 and 1921 belong here, in accordance with the wishes of their families. Patrick Maher will be interred next week in Co Limerick.

This is a day that has been sought for many years, with the support of successive Governments. All of us wished this to be a unifying occasion, in accordance with the wishes of the families today, who have assented to the re-interment. The men we honour belong to a period, when the entire national movement was united in a tremendous effort to achieve Ireland's independence that was desired and voted for by a large majority of the people. War, for whatever cause and whatever circumstances, always has cruel consequences. But every nation, both large and small, has a right to defend and vindicate its freedom in accordance with the will of its people. If an Irish national democracy could have been established peacefully, through elections, or by passive resistance, that would have been preferable. But a realistic reading of history shows government determination to prevent that, by force, if necessary.

The 10 Volunteers executed in Mountjoy died defending and upholding the independence proclaimed by Dáil Éireann on 21 January 1919. The British government of the day, who would relinquish control of this part of Ireland in 1922, were seeking in vain to maintain their continued rule by force, long after popular consent had been definitively withdrawn. Erskine Childers, who with Desmond FitzGerald was charged with explaining the Irish case to a wider international audience, stated that Kevin Barry was doing precisely what Englishmen would be doing under the same circumstances and under the same provocation, and that what was involved was a national uprising, 'a collision between two governments, one resting on consent, the other on force'.

The area of Ireland outside of six Ulster counties, having rejected the limited home rule offered by the Government of Ireland Act 1920, was ruled by a crown colony form of government with martial law declared in many places. The situation was not greatly different from that of the 13 colonies, that went on to form the United States, when they decided to throw off tyranny in 1776. George Washington was a soldier-statesman, and the American War of Independence was one of the principal inspirations of the independence struggle, led by New York-born Eamon de Valera, Cork-born Michael Collins, who had worked for some years in London, and Arthur Griffith, the founder of Sinn Féin. The Irish struggle was a legitimate inspiration to national independence movements in the colonies of the European Empires, and in many cases curtailed the sacrifices for freedom that colonised peoples elsewhere would have to make. The Indian Congress leader, Nehru, wrote letters from prison about Ireland's independence struggle to his daughter, Indira, in the 1930s. Ireland has a right to be proud of its role in the liberation of oppressed peoples around the world, which has given us a continuing empathy with countries struggling to achieve peace and higher development.

Before the Truce, the Dáil, and the Government, all members of the Dáil, took formal responsibility as the elected representatives of the people for the actions of the Volunteers, and recognised them as their army. They explicitly acknowledged the democratic legitimacy of the campaign that they had fought, and accepted accountability for it. So those of us who are proud of our national independence should have no reservations about honouring those Volunteers. On the other hand, it would be quite wrong to apply without distinction, any such presumption to other times and circumstances, and to a quite different situation, or to stretch the democratic mandate of 1918 far beyond its natural term. Conversely, the memory of the Volunteers of 1920 and 1921 does not deserve to be burdened with responsibility for terrible deeds or the actions of tiny minorities that happened long after their deaths. People of common sense and goodwill understand all of that perfectly.

How the principle of self-determination was to be applied, particularly in local situations where majority and the minority were different from elsewhere in the country, was open to argument.

But by 1920 it was accepted everywhere that a locally strong minority could not be allowed to block indefinitely self-government in the rest of Ireland. Not everyone on this island, then or now, sympathised with, or supported, Ireland's independence as a separate and self-governing country. Minorities within came to accept and give loyalty to the State, and in time a broader pluralistic culture in place of toleration has developed. The ideals and experiences of Irish-Ireland and of Ulster Unionism were so far apart, as to make mutual comprehension difficult. Irish Nationalism itself took many legitimate forms, including the honourable, constitutional tradition, going back to Daniel O'Connell, which had greatly advanced the cause of self-government.

In 1918, Sinn Féin and the Irish Parliamentary Party, Eamon de Valera and John Dillon, stood on the same platforms opposing conscription.

The Government of Ireland Act, 1920, was never accepted in the South, but was not a satisfactory settlement for anybody, other than the unionist community, even in the area designated as Northern Ireland, where it was implemented. Today, it is gone. Revisiting the problem of relations between North and South and between the islands, and creating a new, just and equitable system of democratic government throughout the island, has been the difficult task that our generation has had to take up, after much trauma. The Good Friday Agreement has moved us to a new stage in our history, but that certainly does not mean we forget or repudiate those who founded our State.

This State has abolished the death penalty, and lives by the rule of law. There is neither need nor excuse for the extra-judicial use of force by anyone today. The same is true of Northern Ireland, and beyond dispute since the Good Friday agreement.

Today's ceremonies relate to the circumstances that led to the foundation of this State, and the sacrifices involved. We have much to be proud of, and the achievement, however incomplete, is considerable. We all look to a future in which the people of Ireland can conduct warm and friendly relations with each other and with our neighbours in Great Britain on a basis of equality and partnership, in an atmosphere free of force and coercion, and in which people of all traditions can live and co-operate together for the common good.[12]

The tricolour was raised from half mast to full mast. The playing of the national anthem marked the end of the ceremony.

On Friday 19 October at 1 p.m., Patrick Maher's cortège left Sarsfield Barracks in Limerick under Garda escort. The cortège halted outside Limerick Jail where Maher and Foley had been held for a time. A prison guard of honour gave a salute. The cortège then passed through several villages before arriving in Galbally, where there was a ceremony at the monument to the Galbally Volunteers. The cortège proceeded to Knocklong Station (where the rescue of Sean Hogan had taken place in May 1919) where children from Knocklong National School acted as guard of honour and the Proclamation was read by Geraldine Quinlan, a relative of Patrick Maher. En route to Glenbrohane church it stopped briefly outside Maher's home. Arriving at the church a lone piper played a lament. Children from Glenbrohane National School formed a guard of honour. The next day a Solemn Requiem Mass was celebrated by Archbishop Dermot Clifford.

Patrick Maher's coffin before the altar in Glenbrohane church.

After the service members of the military conveyed the coffin to Ballylanders Cemetery where it was placed with military honours in the republican plot. The Minister for Justice, John O'Donoghue, gave the graveside oration, which brought to a conclusion the state funeral of the ten men hanged for Ireland in Mountjoy Prison.

Members of the military remove the tricolour from Patrick Maher's coffin, Ballylanders Cemetery.

A Dhaoine Uaisle.

A cháirde, nuair a bhí ath-adhlacadh na nÓglach á phlé againn i dtosach, socraíodh go ndéanfaí gach rud de réir thoil mhuintir na nÓglach féin maidir le gach gné dá sochraidí. Roghnaigh muintir Phádraig go gcuirfí anseo é ina cheantar dúchais agus sin atá á dhéanamh againn inniu. Tá a ainm greannta ar uaigh Dheichniúr Mhoinseó atá anois le feiceáil i Reilig Ghlas Naíon. Deir feartlaoi na huaighe sin go bhfuil Pádraig ina luí 'faoi fhód glas Bhaile an Londraigh'.

Tá muintir na hÉireann faoi chomaoin ag Pádraig Ó Meachair agus ag muintir an cheantair seo agus geallaim daoibh anseo inniu, faoi mar a dúirt an Taoiseach ina óráid i nGlas Naíon an Domhnach seo caite

- níl dearmad déanta ag muintir na hÉireann ar Phádraig Ó Meachair ná ar a chomrádaithe agus ní dhéanfar go deo.

Dear friends, when the reburial of these Volunteers was being discussed in the beginning it was decided to proceed according to the wishes of the families in all respects pertaining to their funerals. Patrick's people chose to have him buried here in his native place and that is what we are doing. His name is carved on the grave of the Mountjoy Ten now to be seen in Glasnevin Cemetery and the epitaph says that Ballylanders guards his grave.

It is a moving experience for us all to be here today at the graveside of an Irish patriot who gave his life in the cause of Irish freedom. We honour Volunteer Patrick Maher a young man who in the aftermath of 1916, when the Republic was proclaimed, and the meeting of the First Dáil in January 1919 which made a Declaration of Independence, was moved to protect and defend the will to independence of the Irish people. That involved separation from the British Empire and self determination for the Irish people.

We are keeping faith with the wishes of a man, a patriot, and with Patrick's family, as we inter him in his native county.

Those haunting lines from the pen of Francis Ledwidge, who lost his own life at the Battle of Ypres, in his lament for Thomas McDonagh, poet, playwright, teacher, soldier of Ireland and signatory of the Proclamation come to my mind:

> He shall not hear the bittern cry
> In the wild sky, where he is lain,
> Nor voices of the sweeter birds,
> Above the wailing of the rain
> But when the Dark Cow leaves the moor,
> And pastures poor with greedy weeds,
> Perhaps he'll hear her low at morn,
> Lifting her head in pleasant meads.

The land and the people for whom Patrick Maher gave his young life in 1921 has long owed him this honour. It is a rightful thing that his mortal remains should be returned last Sunday in Mountjoy Prison to his family. It is right and fitting also that his body should at last find an honoured place of rest today among the graves of his ancestors in his native parish and in the soil from which he sprang. The land for which Patrick died, in the words of Thomas Davis, '... is no mere sand bank, thrown up by some recent caprice of earth. It is an ancient land, honoured in the archives of civilisation, traceable into antiquity by its piety, its valour and its sufferings.' The proper inspiration of the past is not to imitate it, but to encourage us forward on the path we are now following, building on the progress that has been made possible by the sacrifices of our earlier generation.

We have much to be proud of in our country's past and that includes the life and death of Patrick Maher. Patrick was a son of this parish. Eighty years after his death on the scaffold in Mountjoy Prison his body returns today at last to his own people, to lie in his native place among the fields of West Limerick, to be at rest among those he would have loved and who would have loved him.

There is solemnity and sadness that a young life was taken - as so many young lives across the divide were prematurely ended in those turbulent times - so that Ireland could enjoy peace and live as co-equals with our neighbours.

All countries honour their patriots, who brought into being a free and independent nation-State, where the only sovereignty recognised was that of the people. It is right and fitting that today, at Ballylanders, Co Limerick, we should honour Patrick Maher, whose body has lain in Mountjoy for over 80 years and denied to his family for so long. It is also right and fitting that the fallen dead of the great wars that have ravaged this planet are honoured down the generations by a grieving and a grateful people. It is right and proper that the many young Irishmen, some, no doubt, from this parish who went out to fight for the rights of other small nations should be honoured. It is our bounden duty, and it is our right and privilege also to cherish our patriots, those who gave their lives not for the recruiting sergeant's vision of a liberated Belgium but for the freedom of this small nation, at a time in our history when only through the force of arms could that freedom be achieved.

Some commentators, including those in the *Daily Mail*, have criticised this solemn occasion. I think it is fair to say that the ceremonies at Mountjoy last week, when the families of the fallen stepped forward to claim the earthly remains of their kin, have shown that Ireland cherishes the memory of precious men like Patrick Maher. Terence MacSwiney, another great Munsterman and patriot once said, 'It is not to those who can inflict most, but to those who can endure most, that the victory is certain.' The families of Patrick Maher and the other nine men who went to the scaffold demonstrated that quality of endurance, as they waited patiently for their loved ones to be returned to them.

The *Daily Mail* might ask itself, what right the British Government of the time had to use force to try and suppress Irish national democracy in the making, using men and tactics of which even those who employed them became deeply ashamed. The period is generally seen as a sad lapse in British standards of democracy and civilisation. One might have thought that some in the British media at least would have taken the occasion to regret and lament their own Government's conduct of the Tan War, rather than criticise us for burying with honours the remains of prisoners whose lives were taken against all the rules of war. The editor might care to look up what his rather better informed predecessor wrote in the *Daily Mail* of 15 December 1919 about the Irish struggle – and I quote – 'This is mature, determined, national, disciplined, and above all, intelligent revolt.' I could not put it better myself.

Those who consider any act of commemoration of the founding of our modern state, those who would deny the Irish people the right to pay homage to the men and women who took action to serve and protect the authority of the Dáil, have a partisan revisionist view of history. They make a false link between the actions of the soldiers of the Republic during the War of Independence and the actions of a tiny minority who today have no democratic mandate for their actions and who deal in the currency of terrorism. These commentators would have us believe that acts of commemoration and of homage in some way give succour and credibility to those who have usurped the legacy of the men and women of 1916 and the War of Independence.

I am confident enough to be able to assert that those who worked, fought and died for Ireland in that period were motivated by high ideals, for which they had an overwhelming democratic mandate. They were vindicating the right of the Irish people, as the Proclamation of 1916 asserted, 'to the ownership of Ireland, and to the unfettered control of Irish destinies', a right given validity by the expressed will of the majority of the people of this island in a General Election that was a plebiscite on the right of Ireland to control its own destiny.

Self-appointed guardians of the moral integrity of our nation would have us abandon our patriots to others and engage in some form of mass-amnesia, as if in so doing we would be better able to understand and provide solutions to the tragedy that was the North of Ireland. I cannot accept this, because to do so is to deny us our own history and without history we are nothing. The men and women of 1916 and of the War of Independence were not evil people, bent on the destruction of their neighbours. They were brave patriots who were embroiled in a war, only for the freedom of their country, a war that was foreseen by the First Dáil as inevitable and for which the Dáil, in solemn assembly, took responsibility. We cannot alter that fact and we should not feel that we must apologise for it either. The democratic mandate of the First Dáil was subsequently renewed in a further Election and the struggle for independence continued, legitimised by the will and conscious decision of the people. We would be failing in our duty to these men and women if we were to abandon them to those who seek to legitimise their evil deeds by claiming an unbroken lineage back to the army of the First Dáil.

The Minister for Justice, John O'Donoghue, giving the graveside oration.

The reality is different. All right-thinking people know that in the wake of a short and tragic Civil War the vast majority of those involved in the struggle for independence accepted that the will of the people was for peace and a new path to secure the political, social and economic progress of our country. We cannot speculate on what Patrick Maher and the nine other patriots executed in Mountjoy would have made of the settlement that arose, and it would be presumptuous of us now to speculate as to their views. We can be sure, however, that these men played their part in the struggle for self-determination, clothed in the inviolable armour of truth and justice which had been bestowed by the people. I would hope that, even allowing for the pain and tragedy, and the sacrifices that followed, there would be a sense of achievement - a sense that the onward march of the nation owes as much to these men as it does to those who came before and after them.

It is vitally important, therefore, to place the events of 1921, 80 years ago, in which the Maher family was to play such a tragic part in their true historical context. The December 1918 General Election was perhaps the most significant and decisive contest in Irish electoral history. It gave an enormous and sweeping endorsement for the Irish separatist movement with the Sinn Féin party capturing 73 seats, 6 seats were won by the Home Rule Party and 26 seats were won by the Unionists largely concentrated in the North of Ireland.

The first Dáil consisting of the available Sinn Féin members elected in 1919 adopted a Democratic Programme largely prepared by the leaders of the Labour Movement who for patriotic reasons had not contested the 1918 election but were of course to play a major part in our subsequent democratic development as an independent State. That programme was largely a restoration and restatement of the social doctrine of the 1916 Proclamation. It provided the clear democratic mandate to defend the independent Irish nation.

In August 1919 the Dáil formally assumed responsibility for and control over the Irish Volunteers which would have included Patrick Maher. These men and women by their actions supported the First Dáil's Declaration of Independence on behalf of the Irish people. As the Taoiseach pointed out in Glasnevin last Sunday, in their actions between 1919 and the Treaty in 1921 the Irish Volunteers had a clear mandate every bit as valid and strong as that of George Washington and his comrades in the United States in 1776.

The democratic path is never an easy one. But if there is one connection between the actions of the men and women of the War of Independence and those of today it is that of doing the will of the people. The commitment to the peaceful development of the island of Ireland was legitimised in the votes of the people, on many occasions since the War of Independence. The mandate of the 1919 Dáil has long since expired. Ireland has taken her place among the nations of the earth. In the North of Ireland context, where there is still majority adherence to British identity, the Irish people as a whole have universally adopted the path of dialogue, persuasion and consent in settling issues. The path of dialogue was most forcefully expressed by all of the people of this island in the Referendum of May, 1998, and the adoption of the Good Friday Agreement.

No mandate exists today for those who would invoke the shade of Patrick Maher, Edmond Foley, Patrick Pearse, Thomas Ashe or Kevin Barry to assert the illusory vision of a forced unity, the attempt at which Eamon DeValera insisted in 1957 would ruin national life for generations. A clear democratic mandate commits our Government to the pursuit of peace and reconciliation, and to a just and lasting settlement of outstanding issues by consent. It is not open, therefore, to any group to seek to usurp the names or actions of the heroes of the War of Independence to any cause other than the path of peace. It is not open to any group to seek to ignite the fires of conflict in any part of this island by invoking the names or actions of the soldiers of the First Dáil, because the people, who gave legitimacy to that struggle at that time, have now invoked a new legitimacy.

This Government is and will be relentless in its pursuit of peace for all the people of this island. We know that we have a real opportunity at this time - in our generation - to create a brighter future for all the people of Ireland, based on the will of the people and embracing the two great traditions on the island of Ireland – Nationalism and Unionism. For the first time in two centuries, the two traditions have been working together in the North of Ireland, and between North and South. We in Government will not break faith with the people and we will not permit any other group, elected or unelected, to frustrate what the people of Ireland have expressed as their will. This does not mean that we cannot or should not honour the sacrifices made by Patrick Maher and his comrades who, in their time, did all that could be done to achieve self-determination for our people in the face of a foreign power which did not recognise the will of the Irish people in any other way.

As the Taoiseach said last Sunday at Glasnevin cemetery the sacrifice of men like Patrick Maher will never be forgotten by the people of Ireland. But, the Taoiseach also acknowledged, as I do now, that Irish Nationalism took many other legitimate forms, including the constitutional traditions of Daniel O'Connell, of the Irish Parliamentary Party, of Parnell and others. All these forms have welded together so that we now enjoy one of the most stable political systems in Europe and for that we should be grateful to those people on all sides who, following the struggle for independence and a tragic Civil War, recognised that the only way forward from there was by engaging in democratic politics, in line with the wishes of the vast majority of people.

Patrick Maher met his death on the scaffold. I take no small amount of pride in the fact that I am the Minister for Justice, Equality and Law Reform in the Irish Government which sought and received the mandate of the people to abolish the death penalty forever. I believe it is a sign of the real coming of age of a nation that it can, with confidence, enshrine as a principle in its constitution that State execution is not acceptable and should not be allowed to take place.

Patrick Maher and his comrades choose an honourable path to fight for the right of Ireland to be free. We remember too, the many

Irishmen who choose another courageous path, whose motives are summed up in the words of another Irishman, poet and soldier, Thomas Kettle.

> Know that we the fools, now with the foolish dead,
> Died not for flag, nor King, nor Emperor,
> But for a dream, born in a herdsman's shed,
> And for the secret scripture of the poor.

Thomas Kettle died at the Battle of the Somme in 1916, along with thousands of Irishmen, many of them Nationalists and Volunteers, who fought together for the rights of small nations. We do not belittle the memory of those brave men by honouring here today a comrade, a fellow countryman, who followed his own conscience and who fought to defend the liberty of this small nation.

Saighdiúr ar son na hÉireann ab ea Patrick Maher. Ní bheidh a leithéid arís ann. Suaimhneas síoraí dá anam dílis cróga.[13]

Notes to the text

1. GPB 1921, 10594.

2. Department of the Taoiseach Papers, S 8904, National Archives.

3. Ibid.

4. Ibid.

5. Ibid.

6. National Graves Association.

7. Department of Justice (Prison Service), Mountjoy Prison, 1920–21 Graves file.

8. Author's collection.

9. *Irish Times*, 9 October 1961.

10. Department of Justice (Prison Service), Mountjoy Prison, 1920–21 Graves file.

11. Catholic Communications Office.

12. Department of Justice (Prison Service), Mountjoy Prison, 1920–21 Graves file.

13. Department of Justice, Equality and Law Reform.

Bibliography

1. Newspapers

Freeman's Journal
Irish Times
Irish Bulletin
Irish Independent
Waterfront News

2. Letters and writings of the ten

Barry, Doyle, Foley, Moran, Ryan and Traynor families.
Kilmainham Gaol and Museum – Thomas Bryan, Frank Flood, Thomas Traynor,
Thomas Whelan.
Fr Fergal MacDonagh

3. House of Lords

Lloyd George Papers
F31/1/30, F/180/5/14, F/180/5/17.

4. National Archives

Convict Reference File 1901 T.6.
Department of the Taoiseach Papers S 8904.
General Prison Board (GPB)
1920 - 9231.
1921 - 2165, 2169, 2221, 2418, 3345, 10594.

5. National Library of Ireland (NLI)

MS 23,409.
MS 31,658.
MS Accession number 5140.

6. Public Record Office

Colonial Office (CO) 904/41, 904/42, 904/43.
Home Office (HO) 45/24753.
Prison Commission (PCOM) 8/212.
War Office (WO) 71/360, 35/88, 71/363, 71/364, 71/365, 71/366.

7. Official Reports

Report of the Committee appointed to review the provisions of the Restoration of Order in Ireland Act, 1920, and of the Regulations made under that Act, HMSO, 1924.
Hansard's Debates of the House of Commons.

8. Books

Abbott, Richard, *Police Casualties in Ireland 1919-1922*, Mercier Press, Cork, 2000.
Beaslai, Piaras, *Michael Collins and the Making of a New Ireland*, Vol. II, Phoenix, London, 1926.
Breen, Dan, *My Fight for Irish Freedom*, Anvil, Dublin, 1989.
Costello, Francis J., *Enduring the Most, the Life and Death of Terence MacSwiney*, Brandon, Dingle, 1995.
Crozier, Brig-Gen. F.P., *The Men I Killed*, Michael Joseph Ltd, London, 1937.
O'Connor, Frank, *The Big Fellow, Michael Collins and the Irish Revolution*, Poolbeg, Dublin, 1979.
Macready, The Rt. Hon Sir Nevil, Gen., *Annals of an Active Life, Vol. II*, Hutchinson, London, 1924.
O'Donovan, Donal, *Kevin Barry and His Times*, Glendale, 1989.
O'Mahony, Sean, *Frongoch: University of Revolution*, FDR Teoranta, Dublin, 1987.
O'Malley, Ernie, *On Another Man's Word*, Anvil Books, Dublin, 1979.
Ryan, Desmond, *Sean Treacy and the 3rd Tipperary Brigade*, The Kerryman, Tralee, 1945.

9. Articles

Donnelly, Simon, 'Escape from Kilmainham Gaol' in *Dublin's Fighting Story, 1913–1921*, Kerryman, Tralee, 1948.
Noyk, Michael, 'Thomas Whelan', *An tOglach*, Winter, 1967.
O'Callaghan, Michael, *For Ireland and Freedom, Roscommon's Contribution to the Fight for Independence*, Colm O'Callaghan, Boyle.
Traynor, Oscar, 'Three Men Walk Out From Kilmainham Gaol' in *Prison Escapes*, Noel Hartnett, ed., Dublin, 1945.